M000238783

Published by CreateSpace, a DBA of On-Demand Publishing, LL

ISBN: 978-1-5136-0734

Copyright © 2015 Craig A. Melby, CCIM

First Edition 2015 Manufactured in the United States of America

*Parts of this book have been adapted from an earlier book, "Leasing Smart," PT Publications, Inc., 1997, co-authored by Craig A. Melby.

Note. This book is available in print and electronic versions.

SITE RITE

*Practical ways to boost profits
with the right site and best terms!*

Craig A. Melby, CCIM

Table of Contents

CHAPTER 3

CHAPTER 4

"What if their locations weren't so good?"

SITE SELECTION & LEASE NEGOTIATION: DO IT RIGHT OR PAY THE PRICE

Choose the best sites:

- What criteria does McDonalds use to pick their sites?

- Why might one side of a street be a good location but not the other?

- What determines whether an additional store or office is needed in a given area?

Know the answers to these questions and you understand the secret of a great location. A location that allows your business to thrive and grow. *By understanding this material, you will make the best possible **site selection** decisions.*

Negotiate the best terms:

- How can you be sure you negotiate the best lease terms possible?

- Are you nervous about personally guaranteeing that ten year lease, and did you take advantage of every possible way to limit your risk?

- Are there any hidden "surprises" waiting for you?

- Did you build in the flexibility you need to allow your company to grow and expand as necessary?

Fact is, NO landlord lease contains all the clauses you should have, and ALL landlord leases contain clauses that should be removed or modified! Understand this and answer the above questions correctly, and you increase your chance of success and limit your risk. *This book gives you the keys to negotiate the best possible lease terms.*

We've been there!

In our capacity as landlord/ property manager and leasing broker, we've seen countless well-meaning and smart business people struggle to make ends meet. Although Joe Pizza Maker produces the best pizza this side of the Atlantic, if he picks the wrong location or makes any of a hundred possible bad lease decisions, his chances for success may be vastly diminished... or even doomed from the start.

Our intention is to give you the knowledge that will increase the accuracy of your decisions and make the sometimes difficult world of business a bit easier.

Business model didn't keep up with the times: Good locations now coming available!

Available space: lease it, or avoid it?

1

LOCATION, LOCATION, LOCATION! HOW TO DETERMINE WHICH IS BEST.

- Why do some major retailers willingly LOSE money for the first few years of operation?

- Why will most successful businesses pay a premium for the best locations?

- Why will some major retailers close a store, continue paying rent on the vacant building, and open up a new store across the street?

"RENT" VS. "PROFIT"
Cheaper rent doesn't mean greater profits

When comparing sites, business owners would be foolish to rely on the dollar amount of rent paid as the primary consideration in choosing a location. The key factor to consider is the NET PROFIT that each location could generate.

While rent may represent a considerable portion of the company's budget, the *incremental difference* between the cost of a poor location and a better location may actually be quite small. When viewed as a percentage of total operating costs, the difference may be quite insignificant, as the following example demonstrates:

OPERATING BUDGET	POOR LOCATION	GOOD LOCATION	PERCENTAGE INCREASE
Rent	10,000	14,000	40 %
Utilities	5,000	5,000	0 %
Salaries	20,000	20,000	0%
Advertising	3,000	3,000	0 %
Miscellaneous	5,000	5,000	0 %
TOTAL	43,000	47,000	10 %

In this example, a 40% increase in rent only increases total expenses by 10%!

In many situations, the total operating costs include a much smaller percentage as rent. Therefore, any increases in rent can result in an even smaller effect on the total expenses. Furthermore, a low cost location with minimal exposure to traffic and customers may increase the advertising budget dramatically in order to offset the decreased customer traffic that a mediocre location generates.

If a higher rent location generates an increase in sales which more than covers the increased rent, then that is an indication of the best choice!

THIS IS CALLED THE SALES TO RENT RATIO

This ratio explains the dollars of gross sales generated for every dollar paid in rent.

	SITE A	SITE B	SITE C	SITE D
EST. SALES	80,000	150,000	190,000	210,000
/ RENT	12,000	20,000	25,000	30,000
= SALES FACTOR	6.67	7.50	7.60	7.00

From this perspective, Site C is the best choice because it should generate 7.6 dollars in sales for every dollar of rent paid. (**Note.** Depending on the gross profit Margin, the business owner may still want to opt for the choice with maximum sales. In this case, Site D will produce $20,000 in additional sales for a $5,000 increase in rent.)

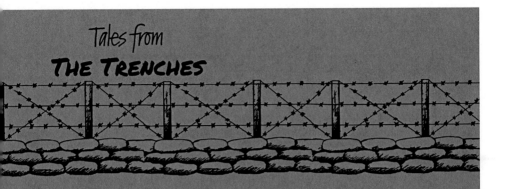

Tales from
THE TRENCHES

GET IT JUST RIGHT.
"CLOSE" IS NOT GOOD ENOUGH

There are countless examples of the heartbreak that comes from putting your time, effort and money into a business, and everything is right except one thing: you picked the wrong location! Maybe by half a block. Maybe only 50 feet - the wrong side of the street even! Maybe upstairs when you need to be ON the street below. "Close" is not good enough.

One of our most successful clients always picked the very best locations and paid the highest rents – for the high visibility and synergy to other anchor tenants. He figured what he paid extra in rent was made up for in decreased advertising. The proof is in the pudding – he continues to open new stores and is very successful. On the other hand, I see retail tenants who pick a "B" location to save some money, then struggle from day one. Breaks my heart. Hopes and dreams dashed. Finances (and marriages) ruined. They should have not entered the business at all.

Do it right, or don't do it at all. Been offered a beautiful location, already built-out with tons of great interior finishes? Hard to resist all this "value"? Don't give in to the lure of beautiful build-out if the location is not JUST RIGHT. Why did the previous tenant fail? (And probably the business before that!) Unless you are a major franchise or business magnet that can change the traffic pattern – stay away.

Here's another common trap: "Coming soon" mixed-use developments with lots of planned residential condos and apartments. Beautiful in their brochures, showing all the happy people living and shopping in the project. Sure, it may happen someday. But the "first generation" of retail tenants are going to have it very rough! The developer wants the stores open as an amenity for their residential sales, but until those residential numbers are there, the stores are going to starve. Demand free rent until a certain amount of people have moved in – which may take years! - and even that may be a terrible deal as you still have to pay for inventory, utilities, payroll, etc. It's no fun running a retail store or restaurant that is empty of customers. This is where the term "second generation" and "third generation" comes from in the commercial real estate business: how many businesses have been here before? Perhaps the third generation tenant will have enough population density to be successful. (PS – it's the poor first generation pioneer who also pays the most in build-out, and "impact fees" which, once paid, are usually not due from future businesses in the space.)

How far did these customers travel to shop here?

ESTIMATING A SITE'S SALES POTENTIAL
Market Demand vs. Competition

Obviously, in applying the sales/rent ratio, great importance must be placed on estimating sales correctly, as errors in either direction will give an inaccurate reading. To accurately estimate potential sales, business owners must analyze both **consumer demand** for their product and the **competition** that is sharing the sales pie.

FIRST STEP IN ESTIMATING A SITE'S POTENTIAL–
Calculating Consumer Demand

Consumer demand is a function of market population, traffic count, or a combination of both.

Demographic reports provide all the information necessary on a given area, however business owners must first determine the size of the trade area, which is usually the DISTANCE customers travel to visit an establishment. For example, food warehouses such as Costco or Sam's Club draw people from 20 miles away (and MUCH further in some rural communities), while a local neighborhood grocery store may only draw customers from a few miles away. A convenience store that sells milk and bread may only draw customers from the immediate neighborhood and rely on traffic passing by for the rest of their volume.

Business owners should take care to determine whether their business is **destination oriented** or **impulse/convenience oriented** and adjust their market reach accordingly. If their business is destination oriented, customers will purposely seek out their services or product. With an **impulse/convenience oriented** type business, customers will visit an establishment while on the

> **"** To accurately estimate potential sales, you must analyze both Consumer Demand and the Competition."

way to or from another destination. The impulse and convenience types of business benefit most by being located in a center anchored by a major chain store thus providing them with a nearby draw or on a free standing location with a strong traffic count. Is their product so unique that their customer will come to you wherever you locate, or are you the best choice because of low price or convenient location?

How do business owners estimate drawing power? Trade associations and franchisors provide them with industry standards for their business type. Existing businesses can also survey their customers directly by gathering information on ZIP codes, telephone exchanges or just asking customers to put a pin in a map. Other business owners outside their market area may also share this type of information.

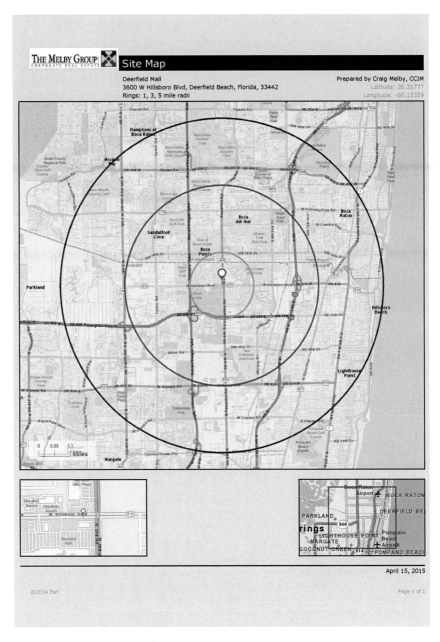

Typical map showing a 1, 3 and 5 mile radius from the site. Because there are no barriers to consumer movement other than interstate and turnpike corridors, this "radius" method works well. However if a lake or river prevented a consumer from reaching the site, then "drive-time" would be a much more valid measure of demographic potential.

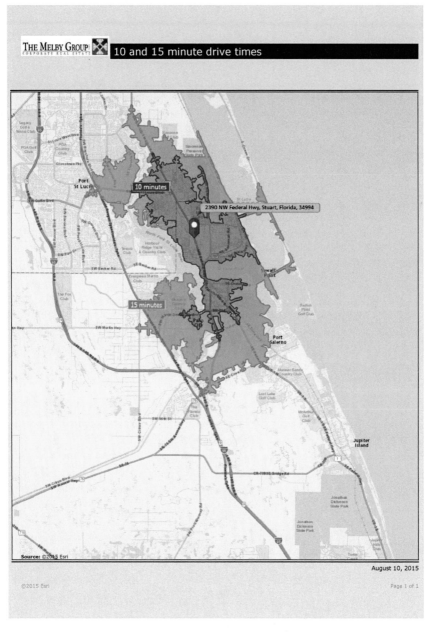

Typical map showing 10 and 15 minute drive times. This "drive time" map is appropriate
for this type geography because of the river separating the population base.

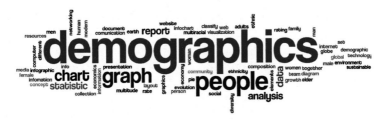

MODERN DEMOGRAPHIC REPORTS – ALMOST MAGIC!

Modern demographic reports go much further than merely reporting US Census Bureau data and updates. Demographic companies now take that information, add surveys from other government and commercial sources, and, in addition to providing standard data about population density and characteristics, they also **make predictions** about how much money will be spent in the trade area, and on which specific category of goods and services.

HOW DO DEMOGRAPHIC PROVIDERS
MAKE THEIR PREDICTIONS?

Demographic companies look at established consumer markets with identifiable characteristics such as marital status, disposable income, net worth, housing values, age, sex, ethnic background and a myriad of other things. Then they look at that group's known consumer behavior, spending patterns and lifestyle choices, and compare those patterns and choices with the demographics of other markets. Assuming similar demographics will create similar patterns and purchasing behaviors, they predict market demand: how much of a certain product will sell, and calculate market potentials and **sales potentials** for given trade areas.

Then they go one step further and estimate **supply**! By using Bureau of Labor Statistics Consumer Expenditure Surveys, Dun & Bradstreet information, sales taxes paid and other commercial and government resources, demographic providers analyze business revenues in the trade area, and look at the gap between the predicted demand and estimated supply. This is where we are introduced to the term "gap analysis". Obviously, a retailer is going to be very happy finding a location where the market is underserved for his type of product.

Following is the first page a typical demographic report showing the most basic demographic information including population density, age, gender and race within a one, three and five mile radius. The full report provides many more details including income levels, net worth, renters vs. homeowners, etc.

THE MELBY GROUP — Executive Summary

Deerfield Mall
3600 W Hillsboro Blvd, Deerfield Beach, Florida, 33442
Rings: 1, 3, 5 mile radii

Prepared by Craig Melby, CCIM
Latitude: 26.31777
Longitude: -80.15359

	1 mile	3 miles	5 miles
Population			
2000 Population	14,049	113,330	293,559
2010 Population	13,449	122,385	307,921
2014 Population	13,685	123,367	311,785
2019 Population	14,484	129,148	327,456
2000-2010 Annual Rate	-0.44%	0.77%	0.48%
2010-2014 Annual Rate	0.41%	0.19%	0.29%
2014-2019 Annual Rate	1.14%	0.92%	0.99%
2014 Male Population	45.9%	47.2%	48.2%
2014 Female Population	54.1%	52.8%	51.8%
2014 Median Age	53.1	44.3	44.0

In the identified area, the current year population is 311,785. In 2010, the Census count in the area was 307,921. The rate of change since 2010 was 0.29% annually. The five-year projection for the population in the area is 327,456 representing a change of 0.99% annually from 2014 to 2019. Currently, the population is 48.2% male and 51.8% female.

Median Age
The median age in this area is 53.1, compared to U.S. median age of 37.7.

Race and Ethnicity			
2014 White Alone	84.8%	75.3%	74.3%
2014 Black Alone	7.4%	14.8%	15.7%
2014 American Indian/Alaska Native Alone	0.1%	0.2%	0.2%
2014 Asian Alone	2.3%	3.0%	2.9%
2014 Pacific Islander Alone	0.0%	0.0%	0.0%
2014 Other Race	2.9%	3.8%	4.0%
2014 Two or More Races	2.4%	2.9%	2.8%
2014 Hispanic Origin (Any Race)	13.8%	18.5%	18.4%

Persons of Hispanic origin represent 18.4% of the population in the identified area compared to 17.5% of the U.S. population. Persons of Hispanic Origin may be of any race. The Diversity Index, which measures the probability that two people from the same area will be from different race/ethnic groups, is 59.6 in the identified area, compared to 62.6 for the U.S. as a whole.

Households			
2000 Households	7,036	52,408	127,231
2010 Households	6,619	53,925	129,420
2014 Total Households	6,691	54,037	130,377
2019 Total Households	7,053	56,359	136,626
2000-2010 Annual Rate	-0.61%	0.29%	0.17%
2010-2014 Annual Rate	0.25%	0.05%	0.17%
2014-2019 Annual Rate	1.06%	0.85%	0.94%
2014 Average Household Size	2.01	2.26	2.33

The household count in this area has changed from 129,420 in 2010 to 130,377 in the current year, a change of 0.17% annually. The five-year projection of households is 136,626, a change of 0.94% annually from the current year total. Average household size is currently 2.33, compared to 2.31 in the year 2010. The number of families in the current year is 76,505 in the specified area.

Data Note: Income is expressed in current dollars
Source: U.S. Census Bureau, Census 2010 Summary File 1. Esri forecasts for 2014 and 2019. Esri converted Census 2000 data into 2010 geography.

Once business owners have a handle on the size or travel time of their typical trade area, they can begin the process of estimating market demand.

Various demographic providers and many commercial real estate brokers have access to a wide variety of demographic reports which become very useful at this point.

Following is a sample of a typical expenditure report which estimates the amounts expected to be spent on certain categories of goods and services within a given region - in this case a 10 mile radius from the target site.

THE MELBY GROUP — House and Home Expenditures

1701 NW Federal Hwy, Stuart, Florida, 34994
Ring: 10 mile radius

Prepared by Craig Melby, CCIM
Latitude: 27.22632
Longitude: -80.26494

	Spending Potential Index	Average Amount Spent	Total
Utilities, Fuels, Public Services	93	$4,603.13	$530,686,062
Bottled Gas	89	$62.11	$7,160,756
Electricity	95	$1,797.86	$207,271,922
Fuel Oil	76	$86.74	$10,000,648
Natural Gas	88	$457.40	$52,732,579
Phone Services	92	$1,509.94	$174,078,271
Water and Other Public Services	99	$678.85	$78,263,487
Coal/Wood/Other Fuel	87	$10.22	$1,178,401
Housekeeping Supplies	93	$658.09	$75,870,370
Laundry and Cleaning Supplies	92	$185.11	$21,341,296
Postage and Stationery	96	$169.60	$19,552,396
Other HH Products (2)	93	$303.39	$34,976,678
Household Textiles	91	$87.61	$10,100,636
Bathroom Linens	91	$11.90	$1,371,926
Bedroom Linens	90	$44.18	$5,093,391
Kitchen and Dining Room Linens	93	$2.31	$266,430
Curtains and Draperies	89	$12.73	$1,467,447
Slipcovers, Decorative Pillows	83	$4.17	$480,266
Materials for Slipcovers/Curtains	101	$11.08	$1,277,296
Other Linens	95	$1.25	$143,880
Furniture	92	$460.58	$53,099,783
Mattresses and Box Springs	92	$85.60	$9,869,226
Other Bedroom Furniture	91	$81.38	$9,381,627
Sofas	91	$118.38	$13,647,837
Living Room Tables and Chairs	94	$60.09	$6,927,847
Kitchen, Dining Room Furniture	88	$35.09	$4,045,873
Infant Furniture	90	$10.70	$1,233,579
Outdoor Furniture	95	$24.46	$2,819,903
Wall Units, Cabinets, Other Furniture (3)	91	$44.88	$5,173,891
Major Appliances	95	$249.34	$28,746,245
Dishwashers and Disposals	95	$20.49	$2,362,629
Refrigerators and Freezers	96	$72.75	$8,386,862
Clothes Washers	96	$43.54	$5,019,403
Clothes Dryers	96	$31.35	$3,614,700
Cooking Stoves and Ovens	95	$34.22	$3,944,732
Microwave Ovens	94	$12.28	$1,415,815
Window Air Conditioners	87	$5.72	$659,030
Electric Floor Cleaning Equipment	94	$20.40	$2,352,418
Sewing Machines and Miscellaneous Appliances	98	$8.59	$990,656

Data Note: The Spending Potential Index (SPI) is household-based, and represents the amount spent for a product or service relative to a national average of 100. Detail may not sum to totals due to rounding.
Source: Esri forecasts for 2014 and 2019; Consumer Spending data are derived from the 2011 and 2012 Consumer Expenditure Surveys, Bureau of Labor Statistics.

January 31, 2015

The following "Market Place Profile" estimates both supply and demand for certain goods and services within a trade area. With this report, Business owners can see whether there is a pent-up demand or an over-supply of the products or services they plan to sell. In this report, the "leakage" indicates the amount of sales being lost to vendors outside the market, since not enough providers are present.

esri · Retail MarketPlace Profile

Proposed Location
100 S Wacker Dr, Chicago, Illinois, 60606
Ring: 1 mile radius

Sample Report
Latitude: 41.88055
Longitude: -87.63701

Summary Demographics

2014 Population	56,942
2014 Households	32,668
2014 Median Disposable Income	$69,393
2014 Per Capita Income	$69,393

Industry Summary	NAICS	Demand (Retail Potential)	Supply (Retail Sales)	Retail Gap	Leakage/Surplus Factor	Number of Businesses
Total Retail Trade and Food & Drink	44-45,722	$1,592,573,834	$2,511,545,368	-$918,971,534	-22.4	1,643
Total Retail Trade	44-45	$1,413,636,408	$1,882,476,057	-$468,839,649	-14.2	1,102
Total Food & Drink	722	$178,937,426	$629,069,311	-$450,131,885	-55.7	540

Industry Group	NAICS	Demand (Retail Potential)	Supply (Retail Sales)	Retail Gap	Leakage/Surplus Factor	Number of Businesses
Motor Vehicle & Parts Dealers	441	$278,645,023	$8,697,713	$269,947,310	93.9	16
Automobile Dealers	4411	$247,564,995	$3,008,606	$244,556,389	97.6	4
Other Motor Vehicle Dealers	4412	$12,364,382	$5,422,660	$6,941,722	39.0	9
Auto Parts, Accessories & Tire Stores	4413	$18,715,645	$266,447	$18,449,198	97.2	3
Furniture & Home Furnishings Stores	442	$31,545,974	$65,930,066	-$34,384,092	-35.3	71
Furniture Stores	4421	$18,923,303	$43,701,706	-$24,778,403	-39.6	49
Home Furnishings Stores	4422	$12,622,671	$22,228,360	-$9,605,689	-27.6	22
Electronics & Appliance Stores	443	$36,839,949	$109,853,232	-$73,013,283	-49.8	67
Bldg Materials, Garden Equip. & Supply Stores	444	$40,061,487	$32,501,591	$7,559,896	10.4	29
Bldg Material & Supplies Dealers	4441	$32,297,994	$31,217,882	$1,080,112	1.7	27
Lawn & Garden Equip & Supply Stores	4442	$7,763,493	$1,283,709	$6,479,784	71.6	2
Food & Beverage Stores	445	$238,435,138	$177,029,156	$61,405,982	14.8	169
Grocery Stores	4451	$210,830,279	$131,626,459	$79,203,820	23.1	101
Specialty Food Stores	4452	$7,094,418	$28,367,509	-$21,273,091	-60.0	54
Beer, Wine & Liquor Stores	4453	$20,510,442	$17,035,188	$3,475,254	9.3	14
Health & Personal Care Stores	446,4461	$121,818,165	$372,809,829	-$250,991,664	-50.7	102
Gasoline Stations	447,4471	$134,842,275	$19,402,845	$115,439,430	74.8	11
Clothing & Clothing Accessories Stores	448	$99,006,111	$222,174,252	-$123,168,141	-38.3	279
Clothing Stores	4481	$70,646,048	$130,674,598	-$60,028,550	-29.8	143
Shoe Stores	4482	$14,892,805	$26,597,148	-$11,704,343	-28.2	27
Jewelry, Luggage & Leather Goods Stores	4483	$13,467,258	$64,902,506	-$51,435,248	-65.6	109
Sporting Goods, Hobby, Book & Music Stores	451	$37,490,635	$40,651,110	-$3,160,475	-4.0	95
Sporting Goods/Hobby/Musical Instr Stores	4511	$28,440,943	$13,548,845	$14,892,098	35.5	52
Book, Periodical & Music Stores	4512	$9,049,692	$27,102,265	-$18,052,573	-49.9	43
General Merchandise Stores	452	$246,998,426	$209,017,059	$37,981,367	8.3	24
Department Stores Excluding Leased Depts.	4521	$92,091,710	$169,504,414	-$77,412,704	-29.6	17
Other General Merchandise Stores	4529	$154,906,717	$39,512,645	$115,394,072	59.4	7
Miscellaneous Store Retailers	453	$29,352,293	$52,797,124	-$23,444,831	-28.5	203
Florists	4531	$1,128,442	$2,110,072	-$981,630	-30.3	26
Office Supplies, Stationery & Gift Stores	4532	$5,106,762	$21,512,889	-$16,406,127	-61.6	57
Used Merchandise Stores	4533	$3,467,175	$4,110,948	-$643,773	-8.5	16
Other Miscellaneous Store Retailers	4539	$19,649,914	$25,063,215	-$5,413,301	-12.1	103
Nonstore Retailers	454	$118,600,932	$571,612,078	-$453,011,146	-65.6	37
Electronic Shopping & Mail-Order Houses	4541	$107,724,851	$539,626,901	-$431,902,050	-66.7	18
Vending Machine Operators	4542	$3,074,968	$1,580,062	$1,494,906	32.1	5
Direct Selling Establishments	4543	$7,801,113	$30,405,115	-$22,604,002	-59.2	14
Food Services & Drinking Places	722	$178,937,426	$629,069,311	-$450,131,885	-55.7	540
Full-Service Restaurants	7221	$75,173,678	$372,285,348	-$297,111,670	-66.4	219
Limited-Service Eating Places	7222	$85,714,375	$179,194,944	-$93,480,569	-35.3	208
Special Food Services	7223	$7,397,577	$33,428,810	-$26,031,233	-63.8	18
Drinking Places - Alcoholic Beverages	7224	$10,651,796	$44,160,208	-$33,508,412	-61.1	94

Data Note: Supply (retail sales) estimates sales to consumers by establishments. Sales to businesses are excluded. Demand (retail potential) estimates the expected amount spent by consumers at retail establishments. Supply and demand estimates are in current dollars. The Leakage/Surplus Factor presents a snapshot of retail opportunity. This is a measure of the relationship between supply and demand that ranges from +100 (total leakage) to -100 (total surplus). A positive value represents 'leakage' of retail opportunity outside the trade area. A negative value represents a surplus of retail sales, a market where customers are drawn in from outside the trade area. The Retail Gap represents the difference between Retail Potential and Retail Sales. Esri uses the North American Industry Classification System (NAICS) to classify businesses by their primary type of economic activity. Retail establishments are classified into 27 industry groups in the Retail Trade sector, as well as four industry groups within the Food Services & Drinking Establishments subsector. For more information on the Retail MarketPlace data, please view the methodology statement at http://www.esri.com/library/whitepapers/pdfs/esri-data-retail-marketplace.pdf.

Source: Esri and Dun & Bradstreet. Copyright 2014 Dun & Bradstreet, Inc. All rights reserved.

September 11, 2014

ANALYZING THE COMPETITION SURROUNDING A SITE

Demographic reports provide estimates of gross sales, current supply, and the gap between the two. For those who want to dig deeper on their own, two measurements give business owners an indication of how much pressure they will face from competition.

SALES VS. COMPETITION &
POPULATION VS. COMPETITION

> #1 - The estimated sales in a given market vs. the number of competing stores in that market = <u>sales</u>/<u>competition</u> <u>ratio</u>.

> #2 - The population within a given market vs. the number of competing businesses within that market = <u>population</u>/<u>competition</u> <u>ratio</u>.

It is easier than ever to determine the competition in a given market. Start with an application like Yelp and ask for the certain type of store in the marketplace, and use Google Earth by using a query such as "drug stores near xyz street address." Then drive the area and physically look at what is there.

Obviously, all stores are not created equal and some stores sales will fluctuate from the average depending on their management and marketing. Since we only need an estimate, we will assume that all stores generate equal sales.

> ✓ *HINT. Look for an area that has a high amount of residential growth but a small amount of commercially zoned land available, as this will limit future competition. Developers of newer communities usually allocate a smaller percentage of commercially zoned land in conformance with strict planning codes. Modern city and county planning departments recognize the blight that comes with allowing too much commercial zoning and the over-building that can follow.*

As an example of the *sales demand/competition ratio*, assume we have access to a study which tells us expected *total consumer demand* of $6,520,000, and we have determined there are 19 competitors. We can now estimate sales per store by dividing the *total consumer demand* by the amount of existing stores in the delineated area.

Total consumer demand	**$ 6,520,000**
/ existing stores	**19**
= sales per store	**$343,157**

The other guideline, and double-check of the sales vs. competition ratio, is the **POPULATION/COMPETITION RATIO**.

For instance, if there are 108,861 people within a three mile radius (size of trade area), we simply divide the amount of people by the amount of stores (19) and get 5,729 people per store. This number by itself is not meaningful but is useful when comparing other sites under consideration.

This is one of the most prized demographics for fashion retailers.

Are these your perfect customers?

TOTAL POPULATION vs. TARGET POPULATION

Sites can be analyzed by using the **total population** or the **"target" population** of the market area. If you have access to the data, you will add to the accuracy of your analysis by using your "target" population. Normally, not *every* resident is a potential customer, therefore a specific "target" market exists that may use particular goods or services. Accordingly, examine the actual profile of the total market population with regards to age, income, etc. How many people or households are too poor, too rich, too young or too old to use the services?

EXAMPLE OF TARGET POPULATIONS

Convenience store proprietors typically prefer a younger, blue collar population. Their research finds that their average consumer has little time to shop, is more convenience oriented, and buys a higher percentage of beer, milk and cigarettes. Therefore, when a convenience store site selector looks at a mobile home park of 5,000 elderly people, he may see no sales potential at all. The reason is that this sector of the population has more time available for shopping and is typically more price sensitive. On the other hand, this site near the mobile home park may arouse a STRONG interest with a grocery store owner if the residents fit the profile of his typical customer.

Business owners can determine the profile of their customer base by utilizing similar methods as were used to estimate their drawing power, or they can do it themselves by:

1. Find an existing location that is doing well, *(yours or a competitors)*, and order a demographic report for that site to determine the size and makeup of the surrounding population. If using a commercial leasing consultant, they should be able to assist with this very easily.

2. On site surveys can be conducted by salespeople and/ or managers.

3. Have customers fill out information cards *(for a contest, drawing, etc.)* and use the information for their studies. Information requested by this form might include distance from facility, age, sex, children, family income etc. *(This type of information is commonly acquired by national retailers when the cashier requests a ZIP code upon check-out.)*

This process of identifying customer base by age, sex, family status, and other characteristics is known as market segmentation.

USING TOTAL POPULATION DENSITY TO COMPARE SITES

After determining the total population of your market and how many competitors are in that market, simply compare the sites under consideration.

Example: Italian restaurants

Beautiful place . . . but how many people live within easy walking distance?

	SITE A	SITE B	SITE C	SITE D
Total population in market	200,000	250,000	120,000	80,000
Square feet of restaurants	80,000	70,000	40,000	15,000
Population per square foot	2.5	3.5	3.0	5.3

In this example we might choose site "D" because there are 5.3 people per foot of restaurants, rather than only 2 to 3 in the other sites.

(In this case we have taken the number of existing Italian restaurants and totaled their square footage. In other instances, like an accounting or legal office, it might be easier and just as effective by dividing the population by the <u>number</u> of facilities to come up with a number of people per office.)

Busy Place! Does your business cater to tourists or locals?

USING TARGET POPULATION TO COMPARE SITES

Assume the most likely customer for our restaurant is 25 to 55 years in age and earns a household income above $40,000 per year. Using a typical demographic report we determine the target populations and analyze the competition's effect on the market.

Example: Italian restaurants (Same as previous)

	SITE A	SITE B	SITE C	SITE D
Target Population in Market	100,000	150,000	60,000	30,000
Square Feet of Restaurants	80,000	70,000	40,000	15,000
Population per square foot	1.25	2.14	1.50	2.00

In this example, we used the same four sites as the previous example, however after analyzing the target population, we decided on site "B". Because we're using the targeted population rather than the entire population, site B becomes more attractive than site D.

NOTHING'S PERFECT–*How Reliable Are Demographic Reports?*

Locating in a high growth area and the demographics don't look right? Check with the post office, power company, phone company and cable company. as they have a good handle on the number of customers for which they provide service.

Seasonal location? A well-known restaurant chain put a new location on the corner of a busy Florida intersection. The traffic count looked great. When summer arrived, they discovered that over 60% of the residents within a mile radius were seasonal residents. The traffic count dropped dramatically!

> **"One thing many demographic reports don't mention: seasonal residents."**

Business owners can find out the seasonality of their customers in a few ways. First, look at the surrounding housing. Does it consist of condominiums or single family homes? Ask a few of the condo managers for the percentage of full time residents. Also check with the area newspaper, since this certainly affects their delivery schedules. Local utility companies encourage their seasonal customers to keep telephone and electric service year round, making the newspaper one of the few remaining sources of this data.

The newspaper's research department tracks both subscriber and non-subscriber households quarterly. They also track the length of the season as well as the length of stay for different residents.

Business owners can apply these percentages for the seasonal months and better estimate gross sales and number of customers for the slower seasonal months.

Lots of traffic . . . but will they stop and shop?

TRAFFIC COUNT AND SALES ESTIMATES

When demographics don't affect business as much as traffic count, we use a different formula to project sales. Say a business owner opens a gas station and expects most of their business is derived from the traffic passing by their location. By using industry data or data from existing stores, they are able to estimate that each customer will spend on the average of $30.00 and about 1% of all cars passing buy will stop in the service station. Average daily sales volume is calculated using traffic count data as follows:

Average daily traffic	**20,000**
times 1 percent stop-off	**.01**
equals daily number of cars	**200**
times $30 average sale	**$30.00**
equals the potential market	**$6,000.00**

When estimating sales from traffic counts, carefully examine the location's accessibility to traffic. Are there median strips preventing cars from accessing the business? Does traffic bottleneck near the location and prevent potential customers from turning into the site? Is exiting difficult?

Foot Traffic. The same formula is used for any business that draws customers from traffic, whether it is vehicular or pedestrian. For example, Tim considers leasing space at a train station lobby for his newspaper stand. About 5,000 passengers ride the train daily. He figures about 5% will buy either a book, newspaper, or magazine from him with an average sale of $5.00 per person.

Average daily foot traffic	5,000
times 5 percent stop-off	.05
equals people per day	250
times $5.00 average sale	$5.00
equals the potential market	$1,250.00

Nothing beats good foot traffic!

HINT. *Another quick source of estimating a good location is to see what the sales are for OTHER establishments in the area. Not necessarily competitors, just other good retailers. If other stores are doing great sales there must be a reason, and it is likely your operation will do fine too.*

CASE STUDY #1. RACQUETBALL CLUB

SITUATION. Joe Smith owns a very successful Fitness & Racquetball Club, "FIT & FUN". His two sons want to expand the family business to include two new "FIT & FUN" clubs which they will manage. Joe has been at the same location for 15 years and knows his trading area and customer base very well. His sons want to stay close to family and friends as well as benefit from the excellent reputation developed by "FIT & FUN", so they will limit their expansion to the surrounding areas.

Joe and his sons have identified their best customers as being singles with incomes over $35,000, and families with children ages 6-13 and incomes in the mid $40's. Additionally, since many of their customers stop in for a lunch workout, they want a strong daytime population. They prefer a location similar to their current place which is in a large, shopping center anchored by a major grocery chain.

SOLUTION. Since, Joe and his sons have lived in the area for many years, they know of the different surrounding areas which would best support similar stores. Accordingly, they pick out four areas, speak with brokers and drive the streets looking for possible sites and note all existing competition.

They, or their broker, call for information on the various sites and request the landlords provide demographic information along with site plans and rental information.

After completing this research, they review the Consumer Demand figures, project Per-Store Sales (based on amount of competition surrounding each site), and Sales to Rent Ratio (based on the quotes given them by various leasing brokers).

They also double-check these sites by calculating the Competition to Target Population Ratio. The choice becomes very obvious, and they proceed with their new locations.

CASE STUDY # 2. AUTO ACCESSORIES

SITUATION. Sam Johnson, swamped with business at his Boston auto accessory shop "CAR STUFF", wants to franchise his business. However, he doesn't know where to franchise or what to charge for different franchise territories without first knowing how many units each territory could support. He DOES know his existing customer base consists of mostly affluent men in their mid-20s to mid-40s. Most of these customers shop at the adjacent upscale clothing stores.

SOLUTION. Sam decides to examine his franchise potential first, and will limit his initial franchise/expansion plans to New England.

FIRST, Sam posts a map of the area in his store and asks his customers to put a blue pin in the spot where they work and a red pin in the spot where they live. After a week it becomes obvious that his customers come from up to eight miles away, and most of them live in the affluent neighborhoods.

He then draws his current trade area on a map and e-mails this information to a demographic company. Within a few days, the demographic company e-mails back the full demographic report on his targeted location. Sam learns that:

- his population base is 86,000 people
- 45% of the population is aged 25 to 54
- average median income is $39,000, 51% female

Sam then orders demographic data for all of the New England area ZIP codes and picks out the locations which match or improve upon his current location. Sam then decides that regions which contain far more than 86,000 people will support more than one store, and he prices the franchise rights for those regions accordingly.

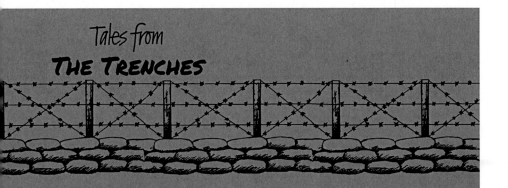

Tales from
THE TRENCHES

DEMOGRAPHICS AS AN AFTERTHOUGHT

Multi-unit retailer: After 15 years in this location, the store's lease was up in 12 months, but they had a renewal option for five more years and intended to remain.

For long term planning we want to negotiate an additional renewal option, and lower future yearly rental increases too, since they seem a little steep in today's market.

I speak to the landlord's broker – real nice guy – and we try to work things out on behalf of our clients. Landlord gets a little persnickety, which leads to tenant taking a hard look at the area, and BING! "Wait a minute. The area around this store has deteriorated over the years, and now that I think about it, my sales here are far less than my other stores. Let's look around at other locations just for fun."

So I perform population density and income-level research within a five mile radius of the store and compare them with the demographics of his more successful stores and the other potential locations. BING ! Turns out we should move! The demographics are clear: higher population densities with higher incomes surround the other locations we can move to and the decision to relocate the store is obvious.

CHAPTER SUMMARY

This chapter provides the tools necessary for site evaluation, and answers the questions presented at the beginning of this chapter.

Q: Why do some major retailers willingly LOSE money for the first few years of operation?

A: *Because they want to "lock-up" the best location, and they know that as the area grows in population, their sales and profits will more than make up for any losses incurred during the earlier years.*

Q: Why will most successful businesses pay a premium for the best locations?

A: *Because these better locations, while costing more, will bring in higher sales and profits and reduce the need for advertising and promotions.*

Q: Why will some major retailers close a store and continue paying rent on the vacant building, and open up a new one across the street?

A: *Because the store's needs change over time relative to store size and layout, which can prompt a move, but they may make a higher profit by paying rent on two locations than to deal with a competitor who might move into their old store and take market share.*

Q: If estimating sales proves to be difficult, is it SAFER to go with the location with the LOWEST rent?

A: *Not necessarily, it could just as easily pose more risk, because a less attractive location may generate fewer sales. In fact, tenant turnover (failure) increases in the lower priced locations. Business owners should never make a decision of this magnitude until they are able to obtain all the information they need.*

" Sales/profits must be the top site selection criteria -- not lower rent. Analyzing the market demand and competition are the best ways to determine the best site. "

2

PHYSICAL FACTORS TO CONSIDER WHEN CHOOSING A SITE - DON'T MESS UP!

- **Why are some shopping centers busy and full, while others nearby have constant turnover and vacancy problems?**

- **Why are some spaces in the same building priced differently than others?**

Once business owners select a market area with the right demographics and a strong customer base, they can choose the specific facility that best meets their needs.

Retail choices range from small strip centers with no anchor store to regional power centers with several anchors. They all have unique characteristics and pricing. Keep in mind that the potential trade area may be based on the distance customers will drive to reach the specific center, and types of centers have different types of draws. For example,

Good spot for a sign, but who will see it?

the neighborhood center which has 30,000 to 100,000 square feet and is anchored by a supermarket will draw customers from 5 to 10 minutes away. Community centers typically have 100,000 to 300,000 square feet of space and house a junior department store or variety store as the key tenant with a supermarket. Shoppers typically drive from 10 to 15 minutes to reach this center. For regional or power centers the drive time increases from 15 to 30 minutes. Regional centers have several department stores or large fashion stores as their anchors and range in size from 300,000 to 1,000,000 square feet.

BUILDINGS HAVE CLASSES

Class "A" buildings feature anchors such as a major department store or other national big box retailers. Although a class "B" center can still provide a good draw, the anchor is usually a regional or local grocery store. The center could also be classified as a type B due to age or condition.

Class "C" space consists of older or outdated centers or those centers with no anchor store.

A building may rate as a class "A" facility today, but it may become a class "B" or "C" in the future. Retail centers can suffer from a design that's become outdated, or they can become inferior because of subsequent factors such as road widening, additional construction, competition, and changing shopping patterns. From multi-million dollar regional malls to the smallest corner office building, a building's life cycle is constantly progressing.

In addition to examining the class and type of center, business owners must take a careful look at all physical features at each potential location. These features include visibility, access, parking, unit placement, dimensions, space size, and utilities.

Corner locations have double the exposure. This design has great room for signage, it's close enough to traffic that drivers will see the store, and walk-by traffic will likely be good too.

HIGH VISIBILITY IS KEY - NOT TRYING TO HIDE ARE YOU?

As a rule, avoid locations with poor sign or store front exposure. Is the business easily viewed from the street or pedestrian walkways? For a start up business, a highly visible pylon sign or store front can greatly increase the number of customers walking through the door. A shop may sell the most delicious ice cream in the entire world but it won't matter if customers don't know that they are there.

KEY CONSIDERATIONS TO BEING NOTICED

Can drive by traffic see the facility or sign easily without causing a traffic accident? How far is the building or sign from the road? Do other buildings, signs, or landscaping block the business store front or sign?

Advertising can be tremendously expensive. On the other hand, a well-placed sign works 24 hours a day, and is typically very effective in bringing in customers.

Ideally, future customers become aware of a business's presence even before they need their products or services. When they DO develop a need, they will already know where to go because of the top-of-mind awareness that has been developed.

Making site-selection decisions from a rendering is always risky . . . how can you be sure of the future pedestrian traffic patterns?

EXAMPLE

Take the case of my veterinarian. His professional image-enhancing sign out front of his office grabs the attention of motorists passing by the building. Although many people don't own a pet, they can't help noticing his sign as they pass on their way to work every morning. As the years go by some people buy pets and GUESS where they go? To the sign they know so well! A better veterinarian may be around the corner, but if the consumers don't know this, it doesn't matter.

While visibility may not matter as much for an office or warehouse user, exposure to the public always helps with name recognition and top-of-mind awareness.

VISIBILITY KILLERS - DON'T MAKE THESE MISTAKES

- Strip centers built perpendicular to the road can limit the visibility for most of its tenants. Except for the fortunate tenant on the "road" end, drive by traffic cannot see the entrances or signs of the other tenants. If a highly visible pylon sign is available for the tenants use, the visibility problem can be reduced.

- "U" shaped buildings provide visibility for only those tenants located on each end and in the middle of the building. The side units limit visibility especially from cars traveling in the opposite direction.

- Spaces blocked by signs, buildings, or landscaping can also limit visibility. Keep in mind that business owners can always check if the landlord could remove the signs or vegetation that blocks the visibility of the space *(providing, of course, that the sign or vegetation in question, is on his site and not on a neighboring property)*.

HINT. *Be careful that "what you see is what you get", and a future building doesn't go up on an out parcel blocking your visibility.*

EASY ACCESS IS VITAL - DON'T MAKE US FIGHT TO COME SEE YOU!

If customers find difficulty in accessing a store as well as pulling out of the parking lot, there may not be a problem. UNLESS, of course, the business has competition nearby! For most businesses, competition is a way of life so they need to make sure that customers find their location convenient and accessible.

The following factors effect access:

1. **TRAFFIC ARTERIES.** Long term road construction near the site limits the number of cars that turn into the building. Maybe a new highway scheduled for completion will bypass this location and make access more difficult. Also notice the location of the medians and highway dividers. Can traffic on the opposite side of the road reach the facility easily?

2. **TRAFFIC PATTERNS AROUND THE CENTER.** How much time does it take driving from one end of the center to the other? Can customers easily get to stores from the anchor without driving through a maze of a parking lot?

3. **ENTRANCES.** All entrances must be clearly marked. Do you notice the entrance <u>after</u> you pass the property?

Breakfast and donut shops provide an excellent example of access preference. These types of businesses insist on being on the "going to work" side of the street so that customers don't inconvenience themselves by crossing traffic! As any driver will tell you, right-in and right-out is the easy way!

If I can't park, I can't stop and shop in your store.

AMPLE PARKING IS MANDATORY!

The above philosophy of customer convenience obviously goes for parking. If customers can't find an easy place to park, don't be surprised if they go somewhere else.

PARKING RATIOS - THE RIGHT NUMBER IS NO SECRET

When choosing a location, look very carefully at the existing parking ratio, commonly expressed as the number of parking spaces per thousand square feet of building. Most municipal building departments require that shopping centers provide customers with a minimum of 4 spaces per every 1,000 square feet of space. They typically require more spaces for office users – usually about 5 spaces for every 1,000 square feet. Therefore, the term "four and a half per thousand" means that there are 4.5 spaces per 1,000 square feet of building *(the higher the ratio, the better)*.

Business owners need to look very carefully at the parking needs of their business and the availability of parking spaces for each location. Keep in mind that some tenants may need parking during the day while others may require more night time parking *(As when a restaurant shares parking spaces with an office building or a movie theater shares parking spaces with a shopping center.)* Make sure that the neighboring businesses do not create an unusual burden on the parking situation. Being located in an area heavily populated by restaurants or by a company who employs a large amount of full time workers could put a crunch on parking needs.

Restaurants require much more parking than most other uses. Usually, the formula is based on the number of seats in the dining area instead of the actual size of the facility. Requirements can differ on other types of businesses as well. Business owners should always confirm the required parking ratio with the proper government authority before they sign a lease.

Large national tenants consider parking very crucial. In fact, they not only dictate the number of spaces the developer will provide, but they even require that the rows be perpendicular to their store's entrance. In this way, customers do not have to walk "across" rows to get inside.

– JULIE CLOPPER / Shutterstock.com

 HINT. *Check to see if the leases for the property can require employees to park away from the store entrances.*

UNIT PLACEMENT - ONE IS NOT THE SAME AS THE OTHER

For retailers, their location *within* the center is very important. Landlords charge a premium for the outside corner or "end cap" units because of the extra visibility and accessibility. Other items that influence placement include proximity to parking and neighboring anchor tenants.

Site prominence leads to top-of-mind awareness leads to more sales.

A relocating business should examine the synergy with neighboring tenants. For example, with a movie theater serving as an anchor tenant, a restaurant or ice cream shop would benefit from the movie theater's foot traffic.

In most situations, tenants should avoid the inside corner of the shopping center because of the increased competition for parking spaces from neighboring tenants and the lack of frontage. If a business chooses this space as their location, a discounted rent should

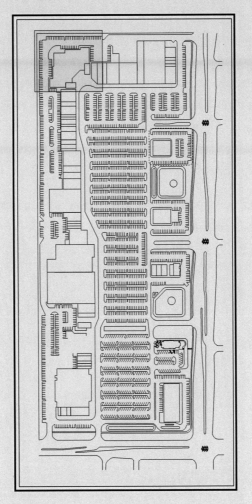

apply. Keep in mind that some businesses such as real estate sales, insurance sales and fitness centers can use corner spaces quite efficiently. For these businesses, the customers and workers stay for longer visits and therefore do not need quick access for parking.

Considering a multi-floor building?

WHICH FLOOR IS BEST? Some tenants require a ground level space that provides easy access for both employees and clients. In the case of sales offices, business owners usually prefer ground level so that their salespeople can get in and out of the office easily. For physicians, the ground level provides easy access for patients, especially elderly or handicapped ones. Some office uses that require single story buildings may prefer locating in a flex building or strip center because it provides them with ease of access along with excellent sign exposure.

On the flip side, some office tenants consider the top level of the building more preferable. The upper floors provide them with a prestigious location and a great view.

Walking by this building? You will only notice the first-floor businesses.

Studies indicate natural light leads to increases in employee productivity, and decreases in sick days.

WINDOWS. Although strip centers and single story flex buildings provide offices with good sign exposure and easy access, they usually lack a fair amount of windows. If associates come in and out of the office often, this may not prove to be an important factor. However, if an employee's job does not permit them to stray away from their desk, studies indicate that the amount of windows and natural light can then affect the productivity and attitude of that employee. A rule of thumb with office workers is the more windows the better.

HEATING /AIR CONDITIONING. The regulation of heating and cooling systems remain a constant problem for many modern high rise office buildings. Be careful about choosing the south side of the building in a region with particularly hot summers. Also exercise caution on selecting the north side of the building if cold winters are common.

GOT THE RIGHT DIMENSIONS?

Primarily a concern to retailers, the dimensions of the facility can impact their business. A long and narrow store may provide ultimate efficiency from a site planning point of view, however, the reduced visibility to customers and lack of frontage hurt the tenant.

Shoplifting may occur more often with a long narrow store since employees may find it difficult to keep an eye on the merchandise as well as the on customers due to the deep store aisles.

Both stores below are exactly the same "size:" 1,200 square feet.

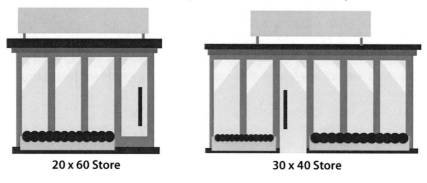

20 x 60 Store   **30 x 40 Store**

(i.e.: A store 20 x 60 deep is the same square footage as a store 30 feet wide x 40 feet deep, but the latter has 50% more storefront "exposure")

SIZE MATTERS - MAKE YOURS JUST RIGHT!

Even if business owners receive low rent and can afford more space than needed, keep in mind the extra costs of utilities and common area maintenance (C.A.M.). Common area maintenance charges, which usually consist of the tenant's pro-rata share of taxes, insurance, and property maintenance are assessed on a square foot basis. The larger the space, the more C.A.M. the tenant will pay. Additionally, a small store packed with merchandise will look far more successful than a large store with empty shelves. "Right-sizing" is the way to go!

An experienced architect or space planner should be consulted especially if the layout consists of more than a basic open bay. Through a well thought out design, these professionals can improve customer traffic flow, position merchandise better, and maximize the efficiency of private offices.

At a minimum, the new business owner should examine the store layout of their leading competitors. *(Walmart's Sam Walton did it all the time!)* By going outside of the market area, the business owner may find companies in a similar business who could offer advice and assistance regarding store layout.

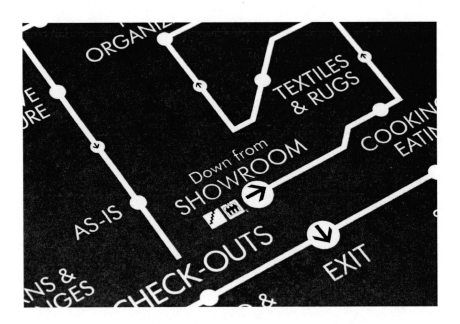

HAVE ALL THE UTILITIES YOU NEED?

Every business needs standard utilities such as electricity, sewage disposal and water. Others need additional utilities such as natural gas. Check if natural gas is already hooked up to the site or if a line runs close to the property. Even if the landlord or leasing broker represents that natural gas is available, the cost of hook up to the site may be prohibitive.

OTHER FACTORS

TRANSPORTATION. Besides providing associates with easy access from the parking lot, highway access is also an important factor. Can sales associates get to major highways easily? Business owners need to examine the transportation to and from work. Do most employees ride the subway or bus? For some businesses, being close to an international airport is a must.

IMPACT FEES. Some governmental agencies charge "Impact Fees" for covering their costs of providing services to growing areas. Impact fees can be assessed by the city, county or state. The charges are assessed for increased use of water, sewer, transportation, law enforcement, schools, parks and recreation. Many times the developer of the property pays these fees at the time of construction, but in some cases the tenant foots the bill. This can even happen with existing space previously occupied by another tenant, specifically when there is a change of use which increases the impact on the local roads, sewer or water systems. These fees can be substantial and concerned business owners may want to check with the local governmental authorities as to the local impact fee situation.

OK, so lets think about this.

PUTTING IT ALL TOGETHER

So what's more important–the layout of the center, location of the center, price, or demographics? There is no clear cut answer. The decision depends upon the type of business. If it is a "destination" business where customers seek you out, then a business owner can consider the "B" or "C" space and benefit from the lower rents and higher concessions. If in the business of selling common products and shoppers have many choices, then a location next to a large department store should increase customer base and thus justify the higher rent.

Tales from
THE TRENCHES

BUSINESS IS HARD ENOUGH WITHOUT PICKING THE RIGHT PROJECT BUT THE WRONG SPOT

We received a call from a company asking about getting out of the disastrous space they are renting. The space is beautiful, already built out by a past tenant, with amazing demographics – all kinds of young, wealthy consumers – just what they like. What could go wrong? Well, they missed it by 20 feet! The location is upstairs, instead of street level where all the pedestrian traffic, impulse and top-of-mind awareness occurs.

Don't think YOUR product is so special that people are going to change their patterns and come visit. Not going to happen. You're not top-of-mind. You're not in their impulse "hey-look-at-that" consciousness. Don't be lured by the siren song of a shiny interior that distracts you from the basics.

CHAPTER SUMMARY

Q: Why will McDonalds open a new store location practically across the street from another McDonalds and keep both open?

A: *Access and consumer demand. The street in question could be a four lane road with a median strip in the center that makes u-turns impractical if not impossible. One side of the street is the "going to work" side that provides the restaurant with plenty of breakfast traffic. The restaurant on the "going home side" would cater to the dinner crowd. Also, there may be enough potential sales in the market to warrant two restaurants in the same market area.*

Q: I'm looking at several different types of centers on the same street. Will all of these centers draw the same amount and type of customers?

A: *Absolutely not! The draw of the center will depend on the type of center (class "A", "B", or "C") or the anchor (or lack of anchor) that occupies the building plus access, visibility and parking. A power center with major department stores and specialty big box stores will draw people as far away as 20 miles. Whereas a neighborhood center may only draw within a few miles. Take a look at the customers who shop at the anchor store and see if they fit into your specific demographic profile. The anchor store manager may also provide more details on the type of customer they attract.*

Q: Why do some spaces in the same building have a different rent than others?

A: *Each space is unique in the center with regard to: visibility, proximity to the anchor, layout of the space, parking availability, etc. Since a center's success depends on the quality of the* *anchor, the anchor tenant will probably pay the lowest amount of rent in the center.   The landlord makes up the difference in profit by charging the other tenants a higher rent, since the smaller tenant benefits from the draw of the anchor through their advertising and notoriety.*

Being in a location with synergistic business that bring your target market to your front door is a good path to success.

" "
When selecting the site,
business owners must examine
ALL the facts: demographics, rent,
type of building and condition,
ingress, egress, visibility, estimated
sales, and customer base."

3

HOW TO NEGOTIATE
THE BEST COMMERCIAL
LEASE TERMS

The first half of this book is obviously directed towards the retail business and making the right site selection decisions. However, since commercial lease negotiation is very similar in all use types, this information will be very useful and valuable to office and industrial users as well, and we will address some of the differences as necessary.

> **HINT.** *ALL landlord leases have clauses in them which should be eliminated or modified, and NO landlord leases contain all the clauses a careful business owner will want added.*

The vast majority of business owners should consider using a commercial leasing consultant or commercial buyer's broker when doing a commercial real estate lease or acquisition. Usually the service is "free" to them since the tenant/buyer's broker is compensated by sharing in the fee the landlords pay to their broker, and the tenant representative's expertise is most often invaluable. Even titans of industry, geniuses in their own fields, rarely know enough about the intricacies of commercial lease negotiations and the myriad deal points and terms unless they deal with it on a full-time basis.

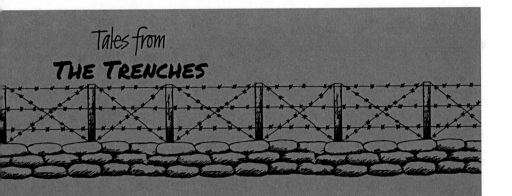

Tales from
THE TRENCHES

NEGOTIATION 201 – HOW NOT TO PUT YOURSELF BETWEEN A ROCK AND A HARD PLACE

An old friend phones and I can hear the tension in his voice. " The lease on my office expires in 2 months, and the landlord wants to raise my rent with the new lease. I think we're paying too much as it is. The new businesses moving in are paying less per square foot than us. That doesn't seem fair."

WOW! A couple of big items here: 1) FAIR is not on the radar. 2) Your TIMING puts you at a huge disadvantage.

Let me explain: the property is owned by a big real estate investment trust. They need continually increasing income so their investors see a nice yield on their investment, or someone gets fired. "Fair" to them is increasing cash flow, year after year. They're nice people, but this is business and they are not your friend. Also: the landlord knows it is EXPENSIVE to move and you are unlikely to do it. Especially with only two months left – you don't have the time! How are you going to lease other space and move within two months? Can't be done. So landlord knows they have you where they want you.

What we did: first, retaining a "tenant rep" was huge. It really shook up the landlord when I called and told them I was now representing the tenant, as the landlord now knows we have researched the market, know what rents are, and know places we COULD move to if we want to. Second, we change the landlord's attitude completely by convincing them we CAN move and WILL move if we have to. We acknowledge it would be difficult, and the tenant would have to work remotely for a short period while new space is made ready, but the effect of too much rent on the business' bottom line and valuation is huge, and we WILL move if we don't come to a more equitable lease.

Result: because we turned the tables and made the Landlord think about the expense and trouble they would have to go through with a big empty space, we get a new lease with the rent LOWERED by $3,000 per month, AND a new $6,000 air conditioner, AND a shorter lease term which the potentially-retiring company owners wanted.

Lesson to all: Timing, timing, timing! Speak with the landlord a YEAR before the lease expires, six months minimum, to negotiate a new lease. Then they'll know you have options, and "fair" may come to the table.

pWhen negotiating anything it is ALWAYS important to be knowledgeable about the subject at hand. In this case, considering the following questions may be helpful:

- What are the best lease terms that can be expected? Being unrealistic is not helpful.

- What are the typical rents and leasing incentives in the marketplace at THIS time? Things are most likely much different since the last time your lease was negotiated.

- What kind of rental rate and terms did the landlord LAST do?

- What makes the situation special?

- How much demand is there for this particular space?

COMMERCIAL REAL ESTATE LEASE TYPES–*You Need to be Clear in Order to Compare Apples to Apples*

The business owner must understand the differences between the different types of leases. The three basic types of leases are **FULL SERVICE, GROSS** and **NET**.

FULL SERVICE LEASE

Used almost exclusively for multi-tenant office buildings, a full service lease is a situation where everything is included in the rent. The landlord pays all of the property's operating expenses including maintenance, taxes and insurance. In this type of lease the landlord also provides the following services:

- utilities including water, electricity, heat and air

- janitorial services

- maintenance services

- security services

NOTE. When using a **full service lease** in a typical multi-story office building, the tenant will be introduced to the concept of Load Factors.

A "load factor" becomes necessary when the tenant uses a certain square footage inside their offices, but also shares in the hallways, bathrooms, elevators, lobby, etc. Therefore, a calculation is done to determine how much of the building's space is devoted to these common areas, and that "load factor" is added to the tenant's square footage. In other words, if twenty percent of the building is devoted to common areas, then twenty percent more footage is added on to the tenant's "usable" area.

GROSS LEASE

In this type of lease the tenant pays the landlord a gross amount for rent, plus sales tax where applicable. The landlord then pays the property's operating expenses such as property taxes, insurance, and management or maintenance costs from the income he receives. The tenant may be responsible for electric, telephone, and possibly water & sewer charges depending on the verbiage of the lease document. This type of lease is more common for office users or in older buildings where utilities may not be separately metered.

> **Example:**
>
> Tenant rents 3,000 sq. ft. @ $25.00 per square foot gross.
> (Assume sales tax is 6%)
>
> | | |
> |---|---:|
> | Tenant square footage | 3000 |
> | Rental rate per square foot | $25.00 |
> | Yearly gross rent | $75,000.00 |
> | Monthly rent | $6,250.00 |
> | Sales tax (assume six percent) | $375.00 |
> | TOTAL RENT CHECK /mo. | $6,625.00 |

NOTE. Some areas of the United States quote their "rate per foot" in MONTHLY terms, so that the above example would be $1.02 per square foot. ($1,276.04 rent / 1,250 square feet)

With some gross leases, the landlord may put an expense stop provision in the lease. In this scenario the tenant pays the excess over a specified ceiling on operating costs. For example, the owner of an office building may require tenants to pay for heating and air conditioning if costs exceed $1.25 per square foot as well as any increases in taxes over those that were paid the first year of the lease.

NET LEASE

Most common with today's commercial properties, the Net Lease directs the tenant to pay the landlord a rental amount that is a combination of BASE RENT plus a share of the property's OPERATING EXPENSES. These operating expenses are usually referred to as "pass-thrus" or "CAM" (Common-Area Maintenance). Many times this is referred to as a "triple net" lease in reference to base rent being "net" of the three main expense pass-thrus, which are:

1. Property taxes

2. Insurance

3. Common Area Maintenance ("CAM")

Depending upon the actual lease document, the "net" rent may also be net of other operating expenses - like roof and structure - and may sometimes be described as an "absolute net" lease.

Net Leases benefit landlords in this way: when the property taxes rise, the tenants pay the increase. When the maintenance goes up, the tenants pay the increase. And so on. With this type of lease, landlords limit their exposure to increased expenses.

Theoretically speaking, a benefit to tenants is that they have more assurance that the property will be properly maintained since monies are collected for that purpose and should not be used for other expenses.

A tenant's share of C.A.M and other expenses is usually based on the prior years of ownership or on a new budget. The landlord usually quotes this as a price per square foot. The pass through expenses are typically paid monthly and can be quoted as "additional rent" in the lease. The tenant may be liable for an additional amount or could receive a credit when actual expenses incurred over the year are reconciled with the amount charged.

From a practical standpoint, landlords seldom credit the tenant for overages. The reason being that landlords typically underestimate expenses when calculating their yearly budget. Quite simply, an overestimate may chase away a tenant while an underestimate may help make the deal.

Tenants should read their lease carefully concerning the C.A.M. charge estimate. Common Area Maintenance, used often as a "catch phrase", may include all the other expenses such as property taxes, insurance, management, etc. Every lease is different so read the lease for the landlord's definition of C.A.M. Make sure the lease clearly itemizes the list of expenses that the business owner is responsible for.

 HINT. Be aware of potential abuse from owner/managers who can raise their management fees and, depending on the lease language, pass the increase on to the tenants. Get the management fee amount agreed to in the lease prior to signing, or have the management portion deleted from C.A.M.

If the yearly pass through cost rises at a rapid rate, business owners may decide to audit their share of the expenses. Other costs, not mentioned in the lease (such as the landlord's personal business expense, company bonuses, or leasing commissions) could have been charged to their account.

When a vacancy exists, the landlord usually pays for the vacant unit's share of the C.A.M., although not always. Business owners should make sure that they are responsible for only their share of C.A.M.,based on the total size of the facility, not just the "rented" portion.

NOTE. "Common area" refers to the areas which the tenants share including parking lot, landscaping, sidewalks, hallways, lobbies, stairwells, elevators and central bathrooms.

HINT. Try to get landlord to put a cap on C.A.M. or any other of the expenses.

Following is an example of how rent is calculated on a net lease.

Assume the following:

- tenant rents a 2,000 sq. ft. store
- total size of center is 25,000 square feet
- base rent is $18.50 per sq. ft. net
- C.A.M., taxes & insurance are estimated at $8.25 per sq. ft.
- sales tax is 6%

What is tenant's monthly rent?

Base rate	$18.50 per sq. ft.
+ C.A.M.	$8.25 per sq. ft.
= total rate	$26.75 per sq. ft.
x tenant sq. ft.	2,000
= yearly rent	$53,500.00
/ 12 months =	$4,458.33 monthly rent
+ sales tax @ 6%	$107.50
	=**$4,725.83 monthly rent check**

If, at year end, the real estate taxes come in $3,400 higher than expected, what will tenant have to pay upon reconciliation?

Expense increase	$3,400.00
size of the center	25,000 sq. ft.
= expense per sq. ft.	$.136 per sq. ft.
x tenant space	2,000
= tenant share	$272.00
+ sales tax @ 6%	$16.32
	= **$288.32 tenant bill**

NOTE ON SALES TAX. In those states where sales tax is due on rent, the sales tax is calculated on the entire amount received by the landlord, whether it is the "gross" amount of a gross lease or the "Base Rent plus C.A.M." of a net lease. There is sometimes confusion from both tenants and landlords when dealing with a net lease as it is sometimes felt that the sales tax should only be charged on the base rent and not on the "expense" portion of the payment. However, since the "expense" portion is included and taxed in a gross lease, most states feel it should also be included and taxed in a net lease also.

SUMMARY CHART OF LEASES	FULL SERVICE	GROSS	NET
BASE RENT	Tenant	Tenant	Tenant
SALES TAX	Tenant	Tenant	Tenant
PROPERTY TAX	Landlord	Landlord	Tenant
PROPERTY INSURANCE	Landlord	Landlord	Tenant
PROPERTY MAINTENANCE	Landlord	Landlord	Tenant
PROPERTY MANAGEMENT	Landlord	Landlord	Tenant
MORTGAGE PAYMENTS	Landlord	Landlord	Landlord
JANITORIAL SERVICES	Landlord	Tenant	Tenant
UTILITIES WITHIN THE UNIT	Landlord	Tenant	Tenant

LEASE TERMS *"Ya get what ya negotiate"*

Now that the major types of leases have been discussed, let's examine the different terms that make up a lease and incentives that are normally negotiated with the landlord.

The incentives offered by a landlord depend on the softness of the rental market as well as the financial strength of the tenant. Landlords will only

Typical example of Common Area with lighting, landscaping and maintenance needs

offer incentives when absolutely necessary. As the rental market gets stronger and more space is absorbed, incentives will tend to decrease. For example, two years ago only 50% of the Village Shopping Center was occupied. The landlord offered 6 months free rent, $10 per square foot in tenant improvements, and rates of $15 per square foot. Since that time, the Village Shopping Center has signed on 6 additional tenants, leaving the center 90% occupied. They will now only offer 2 months free rent, $4 per spare foot in tenant improvements and they increased their asking price to $22 per square foot. Also keep in mind that centers with strong anchor tenants typically offer less incentives than unanchored centers or those with weak anchors.

The actual content and clauses contained in the lease document may vary depending on the type of property, use of the space, lenders requirements, and the insurer's requirements.

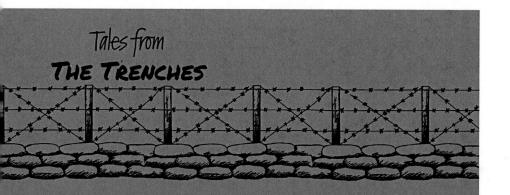

Tales from THE TRENCHES

Ask any landlord, "Should I retain a tenant representative?"

Landlord's answer, "No, because we will have to pay your broker a fee which we will have to pass on to you, so your rent will have to go up if you use a Tenant Representative."

My reply, "Makes logical sense on the surface, except that assumes: a) the tenant representative will not be able to attain a better deal, which they almost always do, b) the landlord is not already paying a commission, which they almost always are, and c) even in the rare instance where a tenant rep does not achieve a better financial deal, they still can be worth their weight in gold by making sure very important terms are addressed in the lease. (Good tenant reps and attorneys work together on your behalf to make sure all safeguards and benefits are achieved.) , and many of these safeguards need to be negotiated at inception, not when the lease is delivered for review and signature. Changing deal terms late in the game can justifiably cause some hard feelings.)

Landlords obviously prefer to deal with tenants who are unrepresented, but are still very happy to deal with a ten-ant rep when they know that is in the cards - especially when the space-search has just started and their first contact with the tenant is through the tenant rep.

Still worried about paying more rent and not getting value from your tenant rep? Tell the landlord YOU will compensate your representative, and pay your tenant rep a percentage of the money they save you. What's to lose? But be warned, the savings may be substantial!

RENTAL RATE

Negotiating the best possible rental rate is probably the single most important item to most tenants and can be one of the easiest assuming the proper research is done!

- What do other tenants in this center pay?

- What was the rent in the last lease that was done?

- What is the asking rental rate for other similar centers in the area?

It's great if the business owner can get all of these questions answered. They may ask the landlord but typically, the landlord will NOT want to answer them. At any rate, it will make the landlord or leasing broker aware that they intend to find out the answers before signing the lease.

When asked these questions, many landlords will then take this opportunity to "level" with business owners. They will explain that, while the asking price is "X", the price they may end up taking is probably about "Y", with the typical concessions of "A, B, C".

In some cases, the asking rent and the final rent may be the same, depending on the occupancy of the property and the strength of the local rental market. However, in MOST cases there will be at least a little give and take on price. One study of office space in the Commercial Investment Real Estate Journal surveyed 79 metro areas and discovered that the "effective rent" (averaged out after taking lease incentives into consideration), was about HALF the "asking rent"!

The very best protection for the tenant in securing the best rental rate is to do the homework. Know what other centers charge and what other tenants pay on this center as well as competing centers. Many landlords will offer this information when asked, but investigate by calling other centers and talking with other tenants. Keep in mind that the rental market is always in a state of change, either getting softer or harder, and yesterday's rental terms and conditions may differ from today's.

> **HINT.** *When negotiating the rental rate, you don't have to argue about what the "fair" market rate is. Simply state that although the asking rental rate is fair-market, YOUR business model will only support "x." If the landlord would like to have you as a tenant, that is all you can pay.*

Storefront looks inviting and you can hardly miss it . . . but where are all the shoppers?

YEARLY RENT ADJUSTMENTS.

During the initial lease term, the landlord could offer a fixed rate over the term of the lease or offer yearly adjustments. The rent can be adjusted by a dollar amount, a fixed percentage or tied to a fixed index such as the Consumer Price Index (CPI).

 HINT. *We like to keep it fixed, or use a CPI increase with a maximum limit.*

TERM

The length of the lease is usually a very important issue. Some landlords may want a long lease for financial stability, or to amortize the amount of money they have spent to attain the tenant. Other landlords may prefer a short lease because of hopes that rental rates may rise in the short term future. Tenants may want a short lease in case of a decline in their business, or reversibly, if their business becomes more profitable and they need more space for expansion purposes. Other tenants may want a LONGER term lease because of an attractive rental rate, a large investment in tenant improvements, the amount of money spent advertising a new location, as well as moving costs if their lease isn't renewed.

Depending on what the landlord wants, the length of the lease will affect all other concessions offered.

 HINT. *Note the "Kick-Out" clause below, which is a way to compromise and keep both parties satisfied.*

"KICK-OUT" CLAUSE

Also known as a lease termination clause, some tenants may want to build-in an option which would allow them to pay the landlord a penalty fee and cancel the lease. A tenant may anticipate future expansion or fear that this location may not produce profitable results for the business. The tenant may also fear that the anchor store may leave, thus significantly reducing traffic flow. Without this clause, the landlord could sue the tenant for all future rents due for the entire length of the lease. This clause can make it less costly for the tenant, who could then pay a set penalty fee and move out.

A typical "kick-out" clause in a five year lease may allow a tenant, after the 24th month, to pay six months rent advance and cancel with proper notice. This clause might also be tied in to a certain minimum gross sales figure that the tenant wants to maintain, or other specific factors.

Landlords (and their mortgage holders) are resistant to allow this clause in a lease. It is possible a tenant will encounter an adamant refusal on this issue.

 HINT. *Kick-Out Clauses will not be found in a typical landlord's standard lease form. This is a clause that must be added by the tenant.*

TENANT Build-out ALLOWANCE

Commonly referred to as "Tenant Improvement Allowance" (*T.I. Allowance),* the developer gives the tenant a certain dollar amount to cover the tenant's cost of finishing the interior improvements, especially in a new, previously unoccupied space. The developer's reasoning is simple: why pour a floor, put up interior walls and ceiling when we don't know the type of tenant that will occupy the space or their construction requirements?

In other words, why risk having to tear out brand new improvements?

Typically, developers of new buildings will finish the space to the point of construction of exterior walls, installation of basic plumbing and placement of electrical service to the unit. The developer then sets aside a certain amount of his construction budget for improvements specific to the individual tenant's needs. This could include such items as drop ceiling, lighting, walls, flooring, private offices, handicapped rest rooms etc. This provides

You might see furniture and a clean layout. We see fire sprinklers, light fix-tures, ceiling tiles, HVAC ducts, wiring, plumbing, flooring, drywall, paint, exit signs, tempered glass and THEN the furniture.

the tenant with the opportunity to design the interior layout to their exact specifications. The TI Allowance can also apply to existing buildings since new tenants typically use a different layout than the previous tenant or the unit may require updating.

If the final cost of the tenant's improvements are above the allotted amount set aside by the developer, they can choose from three options: (1) negotiate that the landlord pay the full amount as part his concession package (2) tenant can pay the amount themselves, or (3) have the landlord amortize the extra amount over the lease term.

When landlords amortize tenant improvements, they may treat part of the contribution as a loan to the tenant. The improvements can be amortized over any length of time but typically are amortized over the initial lease term. For example, say the amount of improvements for a 1,000 square foot space totals $15,000 or $15.00 per square foot. The landlord allows $10.00 per square foot for TI's and will amortize the remaining $5.00 per square foot over the five year lease term at 12% interest. The tenant will in turn pay an extra $111.22 per month towards tenant improvements or an extra $1.33 per sq. ft. per year.

If the landlord provides the tenant improvements, who selects the contractor? Who decides when the work is substantially complete? Who is responsible for the working drawings and permits? Can the landlord make changes in quality of materials without consulting the tenant? The lease document should provide the answers to these questions. Business owners can control the situation better if the landlord provides a build-out allowance and allows the tenant to select the contractor as well as handle all the build-out details.

Most landlords will require that the tenant obtain at least one written bid from a licensed, bonded general contracting company. A tenant may want to receive more than one bid to assure competitive pricing.

NOTE. Many times the landlord will refer to providing the tenant with a "Vanilla Shell" or "Raw Shell". Since each landlord defines the meaning of these terms differently, the tenant should get the finish specifications spelled out in writing. Generally speaking however, the term "vanilla shell" means the landlord is providing the space with four walls ready for paint, concrete floor, ceiling, lighting, bathroom, standard electrical, plumbing and HVAC systems. This would NOT include floor covering, wall covering or any interior partitions.

If the tenant improvements are less than the TI allowance, they may be able to apply part of the credit towards future rental payments or other concessions such as moving expenses.

Building on its way to becoming a Raw Shell. Then comes the water lines, sewer lines, electrical lines, fire sprinklers and HVAC lines . . . all of which are best placed after the Tenant's interior floor plan is designed.

HINT. How and when is the landlord's TI contribution paid? Landlord's first choice is to have the tenant do all the work at tenant's cost, then reimburse the tenant after it is complete. It is possible, though, to get the landlord to contribute TI dollars as the work is being done.

FREE RENT

By offering free rent, the landlord can attract more tenants to the building, especially start-up businesses that need the rent abatement for the first few months of their operation. The amount of free rent offered depends on current market conditions, the vacancy rate in the subject building, and the financial strength of the tenant. The amount of free rent typically ranges from zero to 3 months per year of lease length (a three year lease equals nine months of free rent).

The tenant can use the free rent "upfront" in the first year of the lease. Depending on the creditworthiness of the tenant and the market demand for space, the landlord may insist that any free rent be spread over the lease term. This way, the tenant will not use the free rent period and then vacate soon thereafter. An example would be when a tenant receives every 12th month free, until the credit is depleted.

Sometimes landlords prefer a smaller TI allowance in exchange for more free rent. In this way, the tenant makes a larger capital contribution to the property and is more likely to stay for the length of the lease.

HINT. Make sure the lease specifies when the free rent begins. Some leases will state it commences from the signing of the lease while others specify that the free rent will commence after the construction period and tenant has moved in and commenced business. Most landlords will abate the rent during the construction process and begin the free rent when the space is ready for business. Note that the tenant may pay the C.A.M. charges during a free rent period.

If an anchor tenant vacated the center you are in, would you still be required to remain?

DISCOUNTED RENT

Similar to free rent, discounted rent provides tenants with time to build their gross sales without paying high overhead. With discounted rent, the landlord and tenant agree to a base rental amount and various discount rates during the term of the lease. Typical scenarios would include a reduction of seventy five percent (75%) for the first three months, fifty percent (50%) for the next three months and twenty five percent (25%) for the remainder of the first year.

NOTE. EFFECTIVE vs. FACE RENT

When building owners seek financing for their properties, lenders typically scrutinize the profit and loss statements of their properties. Of course the property owner would prefer to show as much in the way of gross rents as possible. When FREE RENT or DISCOUNTED RENT are offered to tenants, the actual yearly rental amounts are much less than the contract amounts. Since the building's value is based on the actual income received, offering these concessions may decrease the future purchase price or loan amount on that property. That is why landlords would rather offer free rent up-front and charge a higher base rent amount or offer other concessions that would not be as evident on a financial statement.

A rough example would be if a tenant signed a one year lease and agreed to pay $10.00 per square foot "contract" rent. Tenant also received six months of free rent, which is the equivalent of paying $5.00 per square foot for the whole year. Thus, appraisers would use the $5.00 per square foot income, known as the effective rent, when estimating the building's value (and rightly so). The effect of free rent diminishes for longer term leases. For example if the lease were a 5 year lease fixed at $10.00 per square foot, the average effective rent would then calculate to $9.00 per square foot.

The landlord could minimize the effect of free rent by giving the free rent prior to lease commencement. This way, the lease itself does not reflect said "free rent" period, rather, it will only indicate a "tenant fixturing and build-out" period which may not affect the landlord's value as much.

PERSONAL GUARANTIES

For startup businesses and companies with limited assets, landlords may require a personal guaranty of the lease. Usually the owner of the business acts as personal guarantor. By guaranting the lease, the owner can be sued personally by the landlord upon default by the tenant. Tenants should avoid signing personally when possible, although many times it is a non-negotiable demand of the landlord.

Photo taken very early in the morning . . . before the crowds rush in!

HINT. *There are many ways to tweak personal guaranties and reduce the risk to tenant, including limiting the amount of money tenant is liable for, or the number of years the guaranty will cover. Also, check with legal counsel about your state's laws concerning assets and liabilities owned jointly with a spouse and see what protection there may be there if only one of you signs the personal guaranty.*

OPTIONS

Options benefit the tenant, not the landlord, since the tenant can unilaterally choose whether he remains in the building or locates elsewhere. Rather than sign one ten-year lease, the tenant could sign a five year lease with one five year option. The more options, the more flexibility the tenant has in deciding whether to stay or leave.

For the same reason, landlords prefer limits on the amount of options offered because it gives them less control of their property. Some landlords will not give options at all for that reason, but insist on negotiating a new lease at expiration.

Option periods USUALLY have a rental increase associated with them. Typically, the increase may be tied to the Consumer Price Index (CPI) or it may be a prenegotiated amount.

Many times the option rental rate is tied to the "then current market rate". This gives the tenant the right to remain in the premises, while it gives the landlord protection against a below market rental rate. This is obviously in the landlords favor and may be unavoidable.

 HINT. We consider Renewal Options to be "negotiable events"! Tenants should never just give notice that "they hereby exercise their renewal option", without first checking to see if they can get some new incentives, like cleaned or replaced carpet, new or touched-up paint, certain repairs, betters terms, etc.

NOTIFICATION

Usually there is a notification period prior to lease expiration in which the tenant must notify the landlord if he intends to exercise a renewal option. Many times the notification period ranges from three to six months, even longer in some cases. The purpose is to give the landlord time to start leasing the space if the tenant vacates.

Tenants should be very wary of this item. If the landlord wants the tenant out and the tenant forgets to give notice of his intention to stay within the specified time limit, then the landlord may put tenant on notice that the tenant has missed his notification deadline, the option has hereby expired, and tenant should prepare to vacate as of the lease expiration.

HINT. Require the landlord to remind the Tenant of the notification period.

PERCENTAGE RENT

Also known as "overage rent", percentage rent is used most often with retail tenants where the landlord actively promotes the property and thus benefits from the tenant's sales. This is especially common in large shopping centers and malls.

Percentage rent is paid on gross sales that are over and above a certain dollar amount, which is called the "breakpoint". The breakpoint can either be a fixed number or it can be a "natural breakpoint", which floats upward with scheduled increases in base rent.

A "natural" breakpoint occurs when the tenant pays his base rent OR "x" percent of sales, whichever is more.

Formula to figure breakpoint:
Breakpoint = yearly base rent / rate

Example:
Tenant pays $8,500 in base rent per month, and is also obligated for 4% of sales over natural break. What is the breakpoint?

Monthly base rent	$ 8,500
yearly base rent (x 12 months)	$102,000
divide by sales percentage	.04
equals BREAKPOINT	$ 2,550,000

Therefore, the breakpoint is $2,550,000 and tenant must pay 4% of any sales over this amount to landlord as additional rent. (Until the base rent is increased, at which time the breakpoint will automatically increase.)

Using the previous example, if tenant does $2.75 million in sales, total rent will be calculated as follows:

Total sales	$2,750,000
breakpoint sales	$2,550,000
= excess sales	$200,000
x overage percentage	.04
= percentage rent	$8,000
+ sales tax	.06
= additional payment due landlord	$8,480

Typical percentage rental rates change over time and market conditions, but roughly average:

Grocery store	2.5%
Drug store	3.5%
Liquor store	4.0%
Restaurant	4.0%

Percentage rent is usually calculated and paid on a yearly basis since too many fluctuations would exist over and under the breakpoint if calculated monthly.

NOTE. When a tenant leases an extremely prime location, the landlord may retain the right to terminate tenant's lease if the tenant's business does not achieve a minimum amount of sales (and therefore % rent)!

NON-COMPETE–*Don't Try This Elsewhere*

A landlord may require a non-compete clause which will insure that the tenant will not open a similar store within a determined radius or market area. This usually only happens with a percentage rent lease, since the landlord wants to make sure that the tenant is not dividing his market share into two locations, thus diluting the percentage rent.

USE–*What You Can and Cannot Do in the Space*

The USE of the premises is a very important item and should be clearly defined in the lease. The use of the space definitely affects the tenant mix of the center and may directly affect the neighboring tenants as well. If the tenant changes their scope of business or products they sell, the image of the center might suffer. In many retail centers, landlords spend a significant amount of time and money attracting the right mix of tenants to the center that will attract a specific type of shopper. To maintain the

Shopping synergy is very important to both Landlords and Tenants. Ideally, one use complements the other, and there is only one of those uses per center.

center's value, the use must conform to the tenant mix that will most benefit the center. Also keep in mind that the new use may not be compatible with the existing tenants due to the type of product offered or perhaps due to the increased parking requirements, etc.

An additional reason landlords insist of the inclusion of this clause is because another tenant's lease may include the "right of exclusive use". This means that only a certain tenant can sell a specific product or service in the center, thus obligating the landlord to prevent other tenants from selling those same goods or services *(see following section).*

EXCLUSIVITY CLAUSE–*Be the Only One Allowed*

Many tenants desire *(and some REQUIRE),* an exclusivity clause. This provides the tenant with an exclusive right to sell his product or service on the property. *(ex: pizza, eye glasses, insurance, etc.)*

Landlords typically prefer to omit the exclusive right clause from the lease because it takes away their control of the property. However, for strong tenants, most landlords will provide them with assurance that the center

will not lease to their direct competitors. In any case, when the lease IN-
CLUDES this clause, it should be worded very carefully so that the tenant
achieves his desired objective while the landlord is not unreasonably re-
stricted. *(Example: A Chinese Restaurant tenant may request that another*
Chinese restaurant may not be permitted in the Center but the landlord may
lease to other food and drink establishments such as an Italian restaurant.)

ASSIGNMENT AND SUBLETTING–*Preparing for an Unknown Future*

Assignment means that the lessee's rights, title, and interest in the
lease are assigned to another party. While some leases may include the
right to assign the lease to another business owner, restrictions on the
assignability of the lease typically apply. If the lease contains this right
to assign, it is usually subject to the landlord's approval which cannot
be unreasonably withheld. Landlords usually prefer not to allow their
tenants complete freedom to assign their leases, because landlords want
control over tenant mix, and they want to benefit from market rental
rates which may be higher than the tenant is currently paying. If the
lease already contains a strong "use" clause, then the landlord may agree
to include an "assignability" clause. In typical assignments, the original
tenants remain liable to the landlord unless the landlord has specifically
released them.

Subletting means that the tenant leases all or a portion of the premises
to another but still has the primary responsibility to the landlord to see
that the terms and conditions of the lease are carried out in accordance
with the original lease. As with the assignment, the landlord typically
approves the sub lessee. Usually the new sublessee pays rent to the sub-
lessor, who then continues to make payments to the landlord.

 HINT. We always fight for liberal assignment rights so that a landlord
cannot step in the way of a company's mergers and acquisitions activity.

SIGNAGE–*Yours is Beautiful. Theirs? Not So Much.*

While most landlords and tenants agree on the importance of an attractive facility, some tenants feel that constructing the biggest, brightest sign possible is an even higher priority. If every tenant in the center or building constructed a sign with their own specifications, the result would be a hodge podge of signs leading to "sign pollution".

Because of this, most landlords (and municipalities) follow a very specific sign criteria.

The landlord wants a successful building which usually consists of successful tenants, therefore the landlord will probably work with the tenants as much as possible concerning their sign requirements. The problem arises when:

1. All the tenants compete for attention with the largest, brightest signs possible, and the whole property ends up looking terrible.

2. Tenants use different size, quality and style of signs

3. The local zoning department develops restrictions on erected signs.

Thus, discuss specific needs with the landlord, and include exact plans and specifications in the lease. If they are reasonable and within the proper zoning code, most landlords will oblige.

DESCRIPTION OF PREMISES "Useable" Vs "Rentable"

The lease should describe the location in the center, the size of the space and the method used to measure the space, so that disputes don't arise at a later date.

The amount of floor covering required for this space is less than the size being rented. (Useable vs. rentable square footages)

The space that a tenant actually **uses** is termed "useable", while the space that the landlord **rents** is termed "rentable". In most cases usable and rentable square feet differ. The reason being that landlords with shopping centers measure space from the inside of the inside walls and the outside of the outside walls. For office users, landlords may charge a "load factor" or "efficiency factor" that encompasses the tenant's share of common areas such as hallways, bathrooms, etc.

The method of measurement can differ on each competing property. Know what is usable vs. rentable. Most likely the landlord will not change the way the space will be measured and most likely business owners must accept it. However, make sure that all alternative sites are being measured in the same way in order to make a fair comparison.

Example 1: - Typical Retail

Ben Benjamin of Ben's Better Beds rents a store that he has measured very carefully, and found to be exactly 20' 6" wide and 68' deep, or 1,394 square feet. He is surprised when he receives the lease and the rent is figured on a space that is 1,449 square feet. A call to the landlord reveals that the space is being measured from the "inside" of the inside walls, and the "outside" of the outside walls. Since 6" block was used in construction, 6" needed to be added to the front and back dimension, and 3" to each of the side wall dimensions.

Example 2: - Typical Office

Alex Alexander of Ace Accounting rents 2,150 square feet of space in EL PRIMO CONCOURSE OFFICE TOWER. He has estimated his space needs based on the number of employees and office furniture he has, and figures that since he has 1,800 square feet now, 2,150 will give everybody a little more room. The surprise comes when his space planner calls to say that she cannot fit everyone into the new space he is considering. WHY?

Because EL PRIMO CONCOURSE OFFICE TOWER is a very image enhancing, Class A building, and has a large foyer, extra wide hallways, plenty of elevators, a five story atrium, and very upscale, large bathrooms. In fact, of the 100,000 square feet of building, 30,000 square feet (30%) are used up in the above mentioned amenities, leaving 70,000 square feet (70%) of "useable" office space. Therefore, the landlord has added a 30% "load" factor to all of the interior office sizes (70% is the efficiency rating). When Alex deducts this 30% from the 2,150 square feet he thought he was getting, he sees that he only has 1,505 square feet for his business.

Sorry - have to make way for the expanding tenant next door!

RELOCATION–*"You're Moving Me?"*

In some leases the landlord may relocate the tenant to another space if the landlord wishes. Reasons for this include necessary remodeling or the expansion of a neighboring *(usually anchor)* tenant. However from a tenant's point of view this clause should certainly be deleted whenever possible. If the landlord insists on this clause, make sure that he relocates the business to a location with similar sign exposure, frontage, and overall attractiveness of the current site.

"BOILERPLATE"

Standard Commercial Clauses That Make Most Leases So Long

DEFAULT - There are various ways for a tenant to be in default of their lease, such as non-payment of rent, selling goods or services not included in the use provision, not operating during the agreed upon hours, and others depending on the terms of the individual lease.

Many tenants are in technical default for minor reasons, (i.e. an illegal storefront sign, opening up earlier or later than specified, etc.). Typically the landlord will work with business owners to correct the minor deviation and will not seek remedies for default. If the landlord considers the item not important enough to enforce, he may choose to ignore it until it becomes a problem for the center or other tenants.

REMEDIES OF DEFAULT - The landlord will typically want the freedom to use every possible remedy to cure a default, and all possible power to remove business owners from the premises should that become necessary. In normal situations, as long as they pay their rent and follow the basic provisions of the lease, they probably will never have a problem with the landlord. Trying to change too many of the default remedies will be difficult, and may make the landlord very apprehensive when considering the business owner as a tenant.

ESTOPPEL - This simply means that if the landlord sells or mortgages the property the tenant agrees to sign a letter that will acknowledge tenant's current lease situation. Typically this "Estoppel Letter" will note the remaining term on the existing lease, rental amount, arrears if any, and any outstanding charges.

INSURANCE - The tenant must obtain their own liability and tenant insurance for the contents of the space including inventory and tenant improvements. The landlord may specify the specific dollar amount of liability coverage required by the tenant. The landlord will also insure the building regarding liability and property damage. While the landlord's and tenant's liability coverage may overlap, the property insurance covered by the landlord includes everything except the interior contents of the tenant's space. Most leases require business owners to provide the landlord with proof of insurance.

TAXES - The lease should state who is responsible for paying the taxes which may be levied on the premises. With a net lease the tenant pays. Even with a gross lease, any increases may be passed on to the tenant. There also may be some provision for special assessments for sewer, road, or street lighting. Business owners should try to get the landlord to pay for any special assessment charges.

DAMAGE OR DESTRUCTION - What happens if a hurricane or earthquake hits and severely damages the property? Does the tenant continue to pay rent, and for how long? Usually this clause gives the landlord "x" number of days to notify the tenant of his intention to repair and another "x" days to perform the repairs.

HINT. Many standard landlord leases treat this issue inadequately, and force the tenant to return to the property after the repairs are made - even if the time to repair is unlimited! Could your business afford to be shuttered for months while repairs are being done, and if you rented new space to continue operations, are you going to be able to cancel the new lease and return to the old space? Tenants should have a right to cancel the lease if repairs are going to take too long.

REPAIRS - Make sure that the lease specifies who makes repairs to the premises. Obviously, it would be ideal for the landlord to make all of the exterior and interior repairs. Usually this is not the case. Typically the landlord will make major repairs only such as structral items, roof repairs and replacement. Many tenants have not read this section carefully and were later surprised when they experience electrical, plumbing, or air conditioning problems and find that they, not their landlord, are responsible for these repairs and replacements.

> ✓ **HINT.** *Cap the amount tenant will pay per year on HVAC repairs, and/or make landlord responsible for replacement of the units should it come to that. What is the condition of the systems at occupancy? Have the landlord guarantee them for the first 90 days of the lease.*

ALTERATIONS - What happens if the tenant makes major changes to the premises and then vacates, leaving the landlord with an expensive mess to cleanup? What if the improvements do not meet code requirements, or were constructed without permits? That is the reason for this clause. Typically, the landlord simply reserves the right to approve all of the construction work done to the tenant's premises. Tenant shows landlord the plans and permits, landlord gives approval.

The difference between a repair and an alteration should be clearly defined. Generally speaking, a repair is the maintenance of something that was in existence at the time of the acceptance of the leased premises. An alteration, on the other hand, is a substantial change in the leased premises' structure. Alterations could be structural or just cosmetic.

CONDEMNATION - What if the city, county, state or federal government condemns all or part of the property for a road, right-of-way, or utility easement? This clause discusses this issue in detail. Usually landlords' responsibilities depends on the amount of the property condemned, and the effect on the parking area and the physical building. If the condemnation is severe enough, the landlord will usually cancel the lease.

ATTORNMENT - This means that if foreclosure proceedings are brought against the landlord by the mortgage holder, or if a deed is given in lieu of foreclosure, the tenant shall recognize the transfer and accept the new owner as landlord.

SUBORDINATION - This simply means that the tenant agrees that the lease is subordinate to the mortgage. When a new owner purchases the building the leases remain in place and are not affected by the change in ownership. In the same way, the lenders position is not affected by changes in tenant lease situations.

NON-DISTURBANCE - Unless the lender has agreed to a non-disturbance clause, in the event of foreclosure, the lender has the option of keeping or terminating the lease. Many times this term is not in the lease, so when negotiating the lease, business owners may have to have the landlord or their attorney add this clause.

HOLD OVER - This clause specifies the conditions that occur if the tenant stays beyond the term of the lease. This is necessary since the landlord may have a new tenant ready to move into the space when the old tenant's lease expires. Usually, landlords ask for double rent during holdover periods.

✅ **HINT.** *This demand is usually very flexible and many times a landlord will accept a 20% increase instead of their requested 100%. This MAY never matter, but we have seen instances where a tenant's new space is not ready in time, and paying double rent in their old space caused a financial disaster.*

INDEMNIFICATION - What if a tenant falls on the property and breaks a leg? What if the tenant's customer injures themselves while using one of tenant's products or services, and sues tenant and landlord? This clause is designed so that tenants agree not to file suit against the landlord, for any mishaps that may occur at the premises. It usually also states that if landlord and tenant are named in a lawsuit together (perhaps a customer is filing a lawsuit), then the tenant shall pay all landlord's costs in connection with such litigation.

APPOINTMENT OF A RECEIVER - This part of the lease specifies what happens if either the tenant or landlord declares bankruptcy as well as any actions a receiver may take. Keep in mind that if the landlord declares bankruptcy, the receiver could cancel the lease. Therefore business owners should look carefully at the financial strength of the landlord, at least so that the threat of bankruptcy or foreclosure is not obvious.

ABANDONMENT - The lessee generally agrees not to abandon or vacate the premise during the term of the lease. If an anchor store would vacate a center before lease expiration, this could affect the profit of the smaller stores since they rely on the draw of this anchor tenant. Also the insurance rate of the building could increase due to increased exposure to vandalism. Sometimes in retail operations, abandonment is defined on terms of the dollar amount of merchandise that must be available for sale or the amount of hours the store is open. If the store lacks merchandise or is closed most of the time, this will decrease any percentage rents as well as reduce traffic to the center and income of other tenants.

RULES & REGULATIONS - These cover items such as parking regulations, sign requirements, limitations on noise and smell, etc. The rules govern how the business and other tenants must act, being in everyone's best interest.

NOTICES - This section covers how the landlord and the tenant deliver any notices as well as what constitutes a receipt of notice. Notices may be delivered personally, by mail, return receipt requested, or tacked on the door of the premises (the lease will state the method). The lease should specify the time involved with delivery for each type of notice.

RECORDING THE LEASE - In some regions, landlords will record the entire lease or a short form of the lease in the county governmental offices. A recorded lease is considered to be an encumbrance on the property. In fact, in some states a lease over 10 years, must be recorded and for state transfer tax reasons is considered a sale and is taxed as such.

LEASE/PURCHASE OPTIONS

This refers to leasing the building and obtaining an option to buy it during the term of the lease. Especially in a freestanding, single tenant building, the landlord may provide the tenant with an option to purchase. If this

does not cost the tenant any premium in rent or loss of incentives, then why not? (Even if a cost is involved, it still might be a good idea.)

The benefits of the lease/option include:

1. If the building appreciates, the tenant can benefit from the increase in the property's value.

2. Instead of paying rent for years and then renewing their lease, with the right terms, the tenant can convert to mortgage payments and eventually own the building free and clear.

Lease/options can also be made easier through favorable financing arrangements provided by the seller, or when the seller applies a portion of the tenant's rent towards the purchase price/down payment.

It is highly recommended that the tenant use a specialized real estate attorney when drawing up this and other documents. A business owner's attorney may choose one of several ways to draw up the agreement including an option contract, a lease with a purchase contract attached or a purchase contract with a lease attached.

Following is a sample of a simple Net Net Net Lease for study purposes only:

SAMPLE COMMERCIAL LEASE FOR STUDY PURPOSES ONLY

This lease made by and between _____ herein designated Landlord, and _____ herein designated Tenant, acknowledges and bears witness that Landlord does hereby lease and deliver to Tenant, and Tenant does hereby lease, him and accept from Landlord, that certain store space located at _____.

1. DESCRIPTION: That property leased by this instrument is _____ containing approximately ____square feet of floor area measured from exterior surfaces of outside wall and center line of interior dividing walls, together with all improvements including plumbing, electrical, heating and air conditioning servicing the designated space.

2. TERM: The term of this lease shall be for a period of _____ year(s), commencing on _____ and ending on midnight _____ .

3. RENTAL: Yearly Base Rent of $_____ and estimated Common Area Maintenance of $_____ shall be paid in monthly payments as follows;

Base rent	$_____
Common area maintenance	$_____
Misc. (_____)	$_____
Sales tax	$_____
TOTAL	$_____

In the event Tenant's rent payment is received postmarked after the fifth day of the month, Tenant shall promptly pay to Landlord a service charge of $5.00 per day (minimum $30.00) for each day following the fifth of the month that such rent is in arrears.

4. RENT ADJUSTMENT: Base Rental rate shall be increased [ ] a) each year on the anniversary date hereafter, based upon the increase from previous year's "All Items Consumer Price Index" as reported by the United States Department of Labor However, minimum increase to be ____%, maximum _____%. [ ] b) according to following schedule:

5. OPTION: Tenant may renew this lease for _____additional terms of _____ years, provided Tenant gives notice to Landlord of intention to renew no later than ninety days preceding expiration of the original term or any extension term. Renewal rent for the renewal term shall be: [ ] a) increased yearly by _____%, [ ] b) calculated at the then current rate for comparable space in the same market (but not less than the then current rate as annually adjusted).

6. USE: The premises are to be used for the operation of _____ and no other purpose may be used without prior written consent of Landlord. Tenant shall not use any portion of the premises for purposes other than those specified herein above, and no use shall be made or permitted to be made upon the premises, nor acts done, which will increase the existing rate insurance upon the property, or cause cancellation of insurance policies covering said property. Tenant shall not conduct or permit any sale by auction on the premises.

7. ASSIGNMENT AND SUBLETTING: Tenant shall not assign this lease or sublet any portion of the premises without prior written consent of the Landlord. Any such assignment or subletting without consent shall be void and, at the option of the Landlord, may terminate this lease.

8. ORDINANCES AND STATUTES: Tenant shall comply with all statutes, ordinances and requirements of all municipal, state and federal authorities now in force, or which may hereafter be in force, pertaining to the premises, occasioned by or affecting the use thereof by Tenant. The commencement or pendency of any state or federal court abatement proceeding affecting the use of the premises shall, at the option of the Landlord, be deemed a breach hereof.

9. MAINTENANCE, REPAIRS, ALTERATIONS: Tenant acknowledges that the premises are in good order and repair, unless otherwise indicated herein. Tenant shall, at its own expense and at all times, maintain the premises in good and safe condition, including electrical wiring, plumbing, heating and air conditioning installations and any other system or equipment servicing the premises and shall surrender the same, at termination hereof in as good condition as received, normal wear and tear excepted. No improvement or alteration of the premises shall be made without the prior written

consent of the Landlord. Prior to the commencement of any substantial repair, improvement, or alteration, Tenant shall give Landlord at least 2 weeks written notice in order that Landlord may post appropriate notices to avoid any liability for liens.

10. NET NET, NET RENTAL: Except as specifically otherwise provided herein, the basic monthly rental and any additional rent payment for common expenses due by Tenant under this lease shall be net, net, net rental to Landlord, free from all charges of any kind or description whatsoever imposed upon the demised premises or common areas, or which may hereafter arise during the term of this lease or be incurred in the upkeep, operation and maintenance of the demised premises and common area or arising out of the use thereof during the term of this lease.

11. COMMON AREA MAINTENANCE: Tenant shall pay to Landlord its prorata share of the following expenses for services such as, but not limited to, maintenance, common utilities, fire, general liability and lease insurance, management fee, trash removal and real estate taxes and assessments, etc., an estimate sum equal to $_____ per square foot per year of the square footage area leased by the Tenant payable in equal monthly installments due on the first day of each calendar month during the term, in addition to the base rental. If this term shall start on a day other than the first day of a calendar month, then the Tenant shall pay in advance of the beginning date of the term a prorata amount due to the first day of the next month. Whereas said payment for common expenses and maintenance is an estimated figure, the landlord may elect at any time during the term of this lease to readjust said monthly assessment should operating costs and expenses increase during the interim. The Landlord will provide the Tenant with a detailed statement from his Accountant or Auditors, thirty (30) days after the Landlord's corporate year end, outlining all common expenses, maintenance, common utilities, taxes and insurance and any other charges due under this provision and shall either debit the Tenant's account or credit his account for the following year. Should there be any outstanding balance from the Tenant to the Landlord, said sums will be payable within ten (10) days thereof failing which the Tenant will be deemed in breach of this lease and Landlord may take action as per the default clause herein. Should there be any outstanding credit balance from the Landlord to the Tenant, said sums will be credited towards Tenant's next rental payment.

12. ENTRY AND INSPECTION: Tenant shall permit Landlord or Landlord's agents to enter upon the premises at reasonable times and upon reasonable notice, for the purpose of inspecting the same, and will permit Landlord at any time within sixty (60) days prior to the expiration of this lease to place upon the premises any usual "For Lease" signs, and permit persons desiring to lease the same to inspect the premises.

13. INDEMNIFICATION OF LANDLORD: Landlord shall not he liable for any damage or injury to Tenant, or any other person, or to any property, occurring on the demised premises or any part thereof, and Tenant agrees to hold Landlord harmless from any claims for damages, no matter how caused.

14. POSSESSION: If Landlord is unable to deliver possession of the premises at the commencement hereof, Landlord shall not be liable for any damage caused thereby nor shall this lease be void or voidable, but Tenant shall not be liable for any rent until possession is delivered. Tenant may terminate this lease if possession is not delivered within thirty days of the commencement of the term hereof.

15. INSURANCE: Tenant, at its expense, shall maintain a minimum of $1,000,000 in public liability insurance and $500,000 in property damage coverage, insuring Tenant and Landlord. Tenant shall provide Landlord with a Certificate of Insurance showing Landlord as additional insured. The Certificate shall provide for a ten day written notice to Landlord in the event of cancellation of material change of coverage. To the minimum extent permitted by Insurance policies which may be owned by Landlord or Tenant, Tenant and Landlord, for the benefit of each other, waive any and all rights of subrogation which might otherwise exist.

16. UTILITIES: Tenant agrees that it shall be responsible for the payment of all utilities, including, but not limited to, water, gas, electricity, heat and other services delivered to the premises,

17, ABANDONMENT OF PREMISES: Tenant shall not vacate or abandon the premises at any time during the term hereof, and if Tenant shall abandon or vacate the premises, or be dispossessed by process of law, or otherwise, any personal property belonging to Tenant left upon the premises shall be deemed to be abandoned, at the option of Landlord.

18.CONDEMNATION: If any part of the premises shall be taken or condemned for public use, and a part thereof remains which is susceptible of occupation hereunder, this lease shall, as to the part taken, terminate as of the date the condemnor acquires possession, and thereafter Tenant shall be required to pay such proportion of the rent for the remaining term as the value of the premises remaining bears to the total value of the premises at the date of condemnation; provided however, that Landlord may at his option, terminate this lease as of the date the condemnor acquires possession. In the event that the demised premises are condemned in whole, or that such portion is condemned that the remainder is not susceptible for use hereunder, this lease shall terminate upon the date upon which the condemnor acquires possession. All sums which may be payable on account of any condemnation shall belong to the Landlord, and Tenant shall not be entitled to any part thereof, provided however, that Tenant shall be entitled to retain any amount awarded to him for his trade fixtures or moving expenses.

19. TRADE FIXTURES: Any and all improvements made to the premises during the term hereof shall belong to the Landlord except trade fixtures of the Tenant. Tenant may, upon termination hereof, remove all his trade fixtures, but shall repair or pay for all repairs necessary for damages to the premises occasioned by removal,

20. DESTRUCTION OF PREMISES: In the event of a partial destruction of the premises during the term hereof from any cause, Landlord shall forthwith repair the same, provided that such repairs can be made within ninety (90) days under existing governmental laws and regulations, but such partial destruction shall not terminate this lease, except that Tenant shall be entitled to proportionate reduction of rent while such repairs are being made, based upon the extent to which the making of such repairs shall interfere with the business of Tenant on the premises, If such repairs cannot be made within said ninety (90) days, Landlord, at his option, may make the same within a reasonable time, this lease continuing In effect with the rent proportionately abated as aforesaid, and in the event that Landlord shall not elect to make such repairs which cannot be made within ninety (90) days, this lease may be terminated at the option of either party.

In the event that the building in which the demised premises is situated is destroyed to an extent of not less than one-third of the replacement costs thereof, Landlord may elect to terminate this lease whether the demised premises be injured or not. A total destruction of the building in which the premises may be situated shall terminate this lease.

In the event of any dispute between Landlord and Tenant with respect to the provisions hereof, the matter shall be settled by arbitration in such a manner as the parties may agree upon, or if they cannot agree, in accordance with the rules of the American Arbitration Association.

21.INSOLVENCY: In the event that a receiver shall be appointed to take over the business of the Tenant, or in the event that the Tenant shall make a general assignment for the benefit of creditors, or Tenant shall take or suffer any action under any insolvency or bankruptcy act, the same shall constitute a breach of this lease by Tenant.

22. REMEDIES OF LANDLORD ON DEFAULT: In the event of any breach of this lease by Tenant, Landlord, besides other rights and remedies he may have, shall have the immediate right of re-entry and may remove all persons and property from the premises. Such property may be moved and stored in a public warehouse or elsewhere at the cost of, and for the account of Tenant. Should Landlord elect to re-enter, or should he take possession pursuant to legal proceedings or any notice provided by law, he may either terminate this lease or may from time to time, without terminating this lease, relet said premises, or any part thereof, for such term or terms (which may be for a term extending beyond the term of this lease) and at such rental or rentals and upon such other terms and conditions as Landlord, in his sole discretion, may deem advisable with the right to alter or repair the premises upon such reletting. In such event, Tenant shall be immediately liable to pay to Landlord, in addition to any other amounts due hereunder: (a) the cost and expense of such reletting and such alterations or repairs, and any amount by which the rent reserved herein for the period of such reletting, but not beyond the term hereof exceed the amount agreed to be paid as rent for such period; or:(b) at the option of the Landlord, rents received by the Landlord from such reletting shall be applied first to the repayment of indebtedness other than rent due hereunder, second to costs and expenses of reletting and alterations or repairs, and third to the payment of rent due and unpaid hereunder, and the residue, if any shall be held by Landlord and applied in payment of future rent as the same may become due and payable. Tenant shall be credited only with rent actually received by Landlord. Tenant shall, in such event, pay any deficiency between the amount due from Tenant to Landlord and the amount credited. No such re-entry or taking possession by Landlord shall be construed as an election to terminate this lease unless written notice of such intention is given by Landlord, or unless termination be decreed by a court of competent jurisdiction. Notwithstanding any such reletting without termination, Landlord may at any time thereafter elect to terminate this lease on account of such previous breach. Should Landlord at any time terminate this lease for any breach, in addition to any other remedy he may have, he may recover from Tenant all damages he may incur

by reason of such breach, Including the cost of recovering the premises, and Including the worth at the time of such termination, or at the time of an award if suit be instituted to enforce this provision, of the amount by which the unpaid rent for the balance of the term exceeds the amount of the rental loss for the balance of the term which the Tenant proves could be reasonably avoided.

23. SECURITY: The security deposit set forth below shall secure the performance of the Tenant's obligations hereunder. Landlord may, but shall not be obligated to, apply all or a portion of said deposit on account of Tenant's obligations hereunder. Any balance remaining upon termination shall be returned to Tenant within 30 days of Tenant's leaving the premises. The last months rent set forth below, if any, shall be treated the same as the security deposit and, in no event, will the payment of the actual last months rent be excused.

24. ATTORNEY'S FEES: In case suit should be brought for recovery of the premises, or for any sum due hereunder, or because of any act which may arise out of the possession of the premises, by either party, the prevailing party shall be entitled to all costs incurred in connection with such action, including a reasonable attorney's fee, including appellate and bankruptcy proceedings.

25. WAIVER: No failure of Landlord to enforce any term hereof shall be deemed to be a waiver

26. NOTICES: Any notice which either party may or is required to give, shall be given by mailing the same, postage prepaid, to Tenant at the premises, or Landlord at _____, or at such other places as may be designated by the parties from time to time.

27. HOLDING OVER: Any holding over after the expiration of this lease, with the consent of Landlord, shall be construed as a month-to-month tenancy at a rental increase of 50%, otherwise in accordance with the terms hereof, as applicable.

28. TIME: Time is of the essence of this lease.

29. HEIRS, ASSIGNS, SUCCESSORS: This lease is binding upon and inures to the benefit of the heirs, assigns and successors in interest to the parties.

30. PARKING: Tenant shall have a non-exclusive right of use of all parking facilities. Tenant and its employees shall not use the parking areas for storage of any vehicles.

31. CARE OF PREMISES: Tenant and its employees shall not permit, allow, or cause any offensive odors, fumes or gases, smoke, sound or vibration to originate from said premises.

32. RADON: Radon is a naturally occurring radioactive gas that, when it has accumulated in a building in sufficient quantities, may present health risks to persons who are exposed to it over time. Levels of radon that exceed Federal and State guidelines have been found in buildings in _____. Additional information regarding radon and radon testing may be obtained from your county public health unit.

33. RULES AND REGULATIONS: Tenant shall abide by any rules and regulations promulgated by Landlord Continued violation of such rules and regulations after written notice by Landlord and reasonable opportunity to cease or cure shall constitute a breach of this lease.
    A. LOADING: All loading and unloading of goods, merchandise, supplies and fixtures shall be done only at such times, in the areas, and through the entrances, designated for such purposes by Landlord.
    B. ANIMALS: No animals or pets may be brought on or permitted to be in the entire complex without Landlord's prior approval.
    C. ANTENNAS: No radio or television antenna or other similar device shall be installed without first obtaining in each instance Landlord's consent in writing. No aerial shall be erected on the roof or exterior walls of the premises, or on the grounds without, in each instance, the written consent of Landlord Any aerial so installed without such consent shall be subject to removal without notice at any time.
    D. NOISE: No loudspeaker, televisions, phonographs, radios or other devices shall be used in any manner so as to be heard outside of the demised premises.

E. SECURITY: Tenant assumes full responsibility for protecting the demised premises from theft, robbery, and pilferage. Except during Tenant's normal business hours or whenever Tenant is using the demised premises, Tenant shall keep all doors to the demised premises locked and other means of entry secured.

F PLUMBING: The plumbing facilities shall not be used for any other purpose than that for which they are constructed, no foreign substance of any kind shall be thrown in them, and the expense of any breakage, stoppage. or damage resulting from a violation of this provision shall be borne by the Tenant.

G. EXTERMINATION: Tenant shall use at Tenant's cost such pest extermination contractor as Landlord may direct and at such intervals as Landlord may require.

H. SALES: No auction or bankruptcy sales shall be conducted on the demised premises.

I. SALES AREAS: The lobbies, vestibules, sidewalks, and driveways contiguous to the demised premises shall not be used for outdoor displays or sales areas.

J. STORAGE: The demised premises shall not be used as storage or warehouse space for any other business owned and operated by Tenant.

K. SIGNS: Landlord reserves the exclusive right to the roof, side and rear walls of the Premises. Tenant shall not construct any projecting sign or awning without the prior written consent of Landlord which consent shall not be unreasonably withheld. The character, design, color; and layout of all signs shall be subject to Landlord's approval. which shall not be unreasonably withheld.

All signs shall be in accordance with the following requirements:

(1) The sign shall be located within the physical limits of the business front of the demised premises.

(2) No sign shall be located on the roof of the demised premises or the entire complex.

(3) No sign shall project more than 6" beyond the wall on which the sign is affixed.

(4) No sign shall be unnecessarily bright.

(5) All signs shall be fabricated and installed in compliance with all applicable building and electrical codes.

(6) No flashing, moving, flickering, or blinking illumination shall be permitted.

ADDITIONAL RULES: Landlord reserves the right to make such reasonable amendments or additions to these Rules and Regulations as is deemed necessary to the proper administration and care of the entire complex. Any condition existing prior to the creation of a rule or regulation shall not be exempt from the operation of future rules or regulations.

34. OTHER:

ESTOPPEL CERTIFICATE: Tenant shall execute any estoppel certificate requested by Landlord or any mortgagee of Landlord certifying to all material facts relevant to this lease and Tenants possession of the premises. If Tenant does not properly execute and return such an estoppel certificate within 48 hours, then Tenant irrevocably appoints Landlord its attorney in fact, with full power of substitution, to execute such an estoppel certificate on its behalf.

SUBORDINATION AND ATTORNMENT: This lease shall be subordinate to the lien of any mortgage now or hereinafter placed upon the interest of Landlord in the premises. In the event of a transfer to the mortgagee or foreclosure by the mortgagee, Tenant shall be bound to mortgagee to the same extent as if mortgagee were the Landlord under the lease. Tenant agrees to execute any Subordination and Attornment agreement or acknowledgment requested by Landlord's mortgagee. In the event Tenant does not promptly execute or return such a document within 48 hours, then Tenant irrevocably appoints Landlord its attorney in fact, with full power of substitution, to execute a document on its behalf. Tenant's obligation to subordinate this Lease shall be subject to any such mortgagee/Landlord providing an agreement of non-disturbance to Tenant and In no event shall such successor mortgagee have the right to foreclose this Lease so long as Tenant is not in monetary default hereof.

FORCE MAJEURE: Landlord shall not be deemed in default with respect to any of the terms, covenants, or conditions of this lease if Landlord fails to timely perform due in whole or in part to any strike, lockout, labor trouble, civil disorder, inability to procure materials, failure of power, restrictive governmental laws and regulations, riots, insurrections. war, fuel shortages, accidents, casualties, acts of God, acts directly or indirectly caused by Tenant (or Tenant's agents, employees, or invitees), or any other cause beyond the reasonable control of Landlord.

35. RIGHT TO PURCHASE:

Tenant shall have the Exclusive Option to Purchase the Premises known as _____, and which includes the space currently rented to _____, as follows:

OPTION PERIOD shall be after the 24th month, but before the 36th month, of lease commencement.

PRICE shall be $_____ cash or Buyer financing. CLOSING COSTS: Seller agrees to pay for preparation of deed and other documents necessary to perform Seller's obligations under this agreement; excise tax (revenue stamps) required by law; Seller's attorney fee (if desired); cost of preparing and recording any corrective Instruments. Buyer agrees to pay for appraisal; new survey (if desired); Title Insurance Policy; costs of loan and documentation of same; all costs or expenses in securing new financing or assuming existing financing; Buyer's attorney (if desired); recording financing statements. PRORATIONS: Ad valorem taxes, insurance premiums (at Buyer's options), interest, rents, licenses, maintenance fees and any other items capable of being prorated, shall be prorated as of date of closing. In the event the taxes for the current year cannot be ascertained, then rates for the previous year shall be used at closing for prorating taxes with an adjustment being made when the actual amount is ascertained.

RENTAL CREDIT – ____% of Tenant's rental payments paid prior to closing shall apply toward the Purchase Price.

APPROVALS REQUIRED - Because of Tenant's future interest in purchasing the premises, Landlord shall not execute a new lease for the "_____" space without approval of Tenant, which approval shall not be unreasonably withheld.

RECEIVED:

1ST month rent & tax	_____
last month rent	_____
security deposit	_____
miscellaneous	_____
total	_____

ENTIRE AGREEMENT: The foregoing constitutes the entire agreement between the parties and may be modified only by a written agreement signed by both parties. The following Exhibits, If any, have been made a part of the lease before the parties' execution hereof: _____ .

The undersigned Tenant hereby acknowledges receipt of a copy hereof.

WITNESSES

_____

_____

_____
Tenant/Date

_____

_____

_____
Landlord/Date

GUARANTY

Simultaneously with the execution of the foregoing lease, the undersigned jointly and severally guarantee full payment and performance of all obligations of Tenant under the foregoing lease, whether for payment of money or otherwise; make this commitment with intent that Landlord rely upon it in executing the foregoing release; and obligate themselves as original parties without exception, contingency or condition other than that upon payment or other performance by the undersigned guarantors they shall be subrogated to rights and remedies of Landlord against Tenant or such part thereof as may be applicable according to their performance. This guarantee will not be affected by any bankruptcy or insolvency of Tenant and the undersigned acknowledge and agree that; (a) they may be sued directly under this guarantee without first obtaining a judgment against Tenant and without joining Tenant in the lawsuit; and (b) Landlord may allow Tenant to be in default, may extend the time for payment or other performance by Tenant, or otherwise waive, extend, or excuse performance by Tenant without releasing the undersigned from this guarantee.

Provided that Tenant is not in default of this Lease, this personal guaranty shall expire ___ months after Lease Commencement.

IN WITNESS WHEREOF, we have caused these presents to be executed at _____ county, (state), this ____ day of _____, 20xx.

WITNESS AS TO GUARANTORS:

_____

_____

          _____
          Tenant/Date
          Address

_____

_____

          _____
          Tenant/Date
          Address

LANDLORD'S INCOME = LANDLORD'S VALUE

To understand the commercial property investment business from the landlord's point of view, it is important to understand how the property's income effects the value. Put quite simply, the value of the property is basically derived from the rent it produces.

Consequently, both tenant and landlord must examine the different alternatives that allow both parties to reach an agreement on the financial terms of the lease.

Example of building valuation based on the tenant's rent:

The value of a building is usually a relationship between the net income generated, and a yield that an investor typically would receive on similar investments. The yield used by most appraisers and investors is known as the capitalization ("cap") rate. When estimating value, the net income of the property *(after operating expenses)*, is divided by the current market capitalization rate.

For this example, let's assume a 10,000 square foot building generates a yearly net Income of $135,000, and capitalization rates in the marketplace for similar buildings run about 9.5%.

The $135,000 income divided by the .095 cap rate indicates a $1,421,052 value for the building.

$135,000/.095 = $1,421,052

If the landlord received $1.00 more per square foot for this building the net income would increase to $145,000. Using the previous formula, we divide the new income by the cap rate ($145,000 income / .095 rate) and establish a new value of $1,526,315.

Even though the income only went up $10,000, the landlord's value has increased by over $100,000: ten times that much!

Because of this situation, a tenant may find that the landlord will offer upfront lease incentives in order to achieve a higher rental rate. Therefore, if a tenant wanted additional build-out funds over and above what the landlord offered, and if the tenant can afford a bit higher rent, then the landlord may provide the additional build-out funds in order to increase the rent therefore producing a higher property value.

It's great when Landlord and Tenant want the same thing . . . but sometimes that is impossible.

YOUR LEASE OR THEIRS?

Whether tenants use their own real estate lease or the landlord's lease depends on the strength of the tenant. A national anchor will insist on using their own lease while a smaller, local tenant would use the landlord's lease. It is unreasonable for a major landlord to deal with hundreds of different lease forms, and it would also be equally unreasonable for a large national tenant to deal with a different lease for each of its hundreds of locations.

If the landlord does not insist on a standard commercial lease, the tenant should retain the services of a real estate attorney to draw up the lease.

> ✓ **HINT.** *Consider having a standard lease addendum prepared which tenants can attach to the lease and which covers the many special business points important to them.*

Therefore, the lease will contain more of the terms and conditions that the tenant wants from the outset.

Some landlords require the tenant to sign a corporate resolution with their lease document. This document states that the person signing the lease has the authority to do so. This notarized document usually contains the signatures of the president and the secretary of the corporation as well as the corporate seal. For partnerships, the landlord may request a copy of the partnership agreement as well as any addendums that will insure that the party in question can make decisions for the partnership.

As always, it is strongly advised that an experienced real estate attorney be retained to draw up any commercial real estate lease or sale documents.

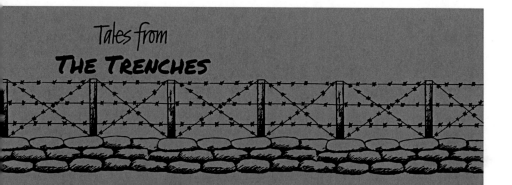

Tales from
THE TRENCHES

NEGOTIATION 101

We are standing in the glittering lobby of a high-rise office building, waiting for the landlord's agent to arrive. I take this moment to quietly tell my client, "Now remember, no matter how much you like the space, don't tell the landlord. We just tell him we are looking at several spaces (true), and will get back to him after our tour. This gives us the leverage we need to negotiate the best deal."

Client looks slightly put off and says, "Sure, no problem"

So the landlord's agent arrives, we go up the elevator and we tour the space I found for him, which I know is perfect for his needs.

As we're finishing the tour, client is getting more and more enthusiastic about what he sees. Turns to the Landlord and says, "This is perfect! What's the rent?"

Landlord's agent tells him the amount.

Client gets wide-eyed and says "That's great – very fair! I'll take it."

OK, so now how am I going to go back and negotiate a lower rent, and get landlord concessions? We've lost some major leverage, and are going to have to do the deal pretty much as-is now that he played his hand face-up. There is no question in my mind that his non-poker face has just cost him a lot of money.

CHAPTER III SUMMARY - SO NOW YOU KNOW THE NUANCES OF ALL THE VARIOUS LEASE TERMS!

In order to compare different opportunities "apples to apples" it is necessary to understand the differences in the types of leases and what services and expenses are included in them.

It is also important to note the various ways of limiting liability, and obtaining the concessions most important to the particular situation.

The bulk of the leases tenants will encounter are similar. It is in the business points where most important differences will occur, and the clauses tenants will want to add to give them flexibility for future circumstances and limit their risk in unexpected situations.

Now that business owners have defined the size of their trade area, they can "hit the streets" and search for that perfect location.

"
Business owners must understand the differences between the different types of leases. The three basic types of leases are FULL SERVICE, GROSS and NET. "

4

GETTING STARTED
READY? SET? GO!
FINDING THE BEST SITES

This is the time for business owners to decide whether to retain professional help or do it themselves. Simply driving the streets in the trade area when looking for possible locations is the first step in finding potential sites if working alone. Most landlords and brokers install signs on vacant spaces, but to learn about spaces that could be MADE available, or are COMING available, business owners should plan to spend some time with a broker describing their needs in detail and leaving contact information.

When a site *does* impress a business owner, they should drive north, south, east and west an appropriate distance to determine:

1. **Population.** What is the population make up of the existing area? Take notice of the type of housing and price range of homes in the surrounding area. Are there mostly apartments or single family homes? Are there enough people close by to support the proposed business?

2. **Competition.** Look around for the competition. How many of immediate competitors exist in the same trade area. If there aren't any, it could be the sign of a good opportunity OR it could mean this market cannot support the product. It's always a good idea to use Yelp, Google Earth and other programs to see what is listed in the area.

3. **Vacancies.** What is the occupancy rate for buildings in this area? If a good portion of the space remains vacant, find out why.

4. **Traffic Patterns.** How many cars per day travel the main arteries in the trade area? Take notice the level of difficulty to reach the various properties in the trade area. Do this on weekends and weekdays - there can be a dramatic difference!

If business owners call on "for lease" signs themselves, they should:

1. Let the leasing broker/landlord know their sincerity and that

No "For Lease" sign in this window . . . but could it still be available?

they are not just another broker or landlord checking prices.

2. Let them know that they are gathering information on all available sites in their trade area. This will illustrate their knowledge of their trade area concerning market prices and terms being offered and provide leverage when negotiations commence.

Tenants should leave their name and phone numbers with the broker or owner. Not doing so will raise questions concerning their sincerity. Also business owners will receive much more detailed information if the leasing broker knows that they have a genuine interest in the property.

DO THE RESEARCH

If business owners are unfamiliar with the commercial leasing market for their trade area, call a few brokers with signs on the commercial properties in the area. Even if the specific properties present little interest to the business owner, these brokers can share their wealth of information about the area and market conditions, and they may know of available (or soon to be available) properties without signs. Since most brokers can represent tenants as well as property owners, it is legitimate to let them invest some time in you.

CREDIBILITY–*You Must Have It!*

When beginning negotiations with the landlord, the tenant should provide the landlord with as many details about their business as possible. The landlord may invest quite a bit of money into the lease transaction including the tenant's build-out, leasing fees, legal fees, etc. The landlord has a right to know into what kind of company he or she is investing. In that regard, the smart tenant should prepare the following five items as professionally as possible:

I. RESUME OF EXPERIENCE–*Show Them How You Know What You're Doing*

The resume should provide the landlord with an overview of the tenant's business experience. After reviewing the resume, the landlord should be confident that the tenant knows how to operate a profitable business.

Tenants should be certain that the resume mentions:

- number of years in business

- success of past/present businesses

- referrals/recommendations from past or current suppliers, landlords, etc.

II. OPENING BUDGET

The opening budget should list all of the items necessary for the opening of the new business venture. This would include build-out costs, advertising, inventory, preopening payroll, etc.

III. FIRST YEAR PROFORMA

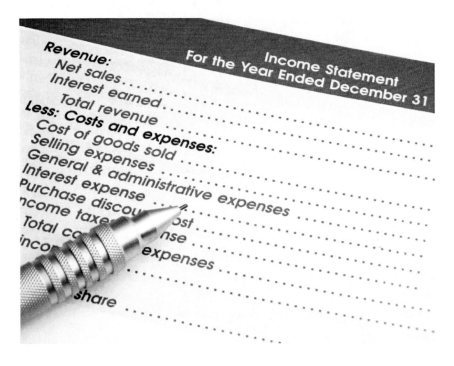

Landlords constantly complain about tenants who open their stores undercapitalized, and with no realistic expectations of the operating costs of their new venture.

True disasters landlords face include:

#1 The hair salon owner who showed up at the landlord's office two days after signing a lease, infuriated at the landlord because he had just now figured out how many heads he was going to have to cut per month just to pay the rent!

This problem was obviously not the landlord's fault as the agreed upon rent was very typical for similar space in that area. Rather, this problem was created by a tenant who had "always wanted to open a hair salon", and decided that signing a lease was the first thing to do.

(This landlord could have stuck to his guns and sued tenant for rent if he refused to proceed, however in this case landlord simply agreed to cancel the lease and find another tenant.)

#2 The cheesecake store owner who stopped in to see the landlord shortly after opening and reported that last month she had "made" $4,000. When landlord inquired whether that was gross or net, the tenant looked confused and replied, "What?"

Landlord then rephrased the question, "Was the $4,000 your sales, or your profit after expenses were paid?"

Tenant replied that the $4,000 was her sales, and that she didn't really know her bottom line. The landlord immediately knew that this tenant was bound for failure, and time proved him right.

IV. BUSINESS PLAN

Many landlords may not require this, but business owners should have one anyway, and have an executive summary ready to share if landlord requests it.

V. FINANCIAL STATEMENT

While the landlord may not require the tenant to submit most of the documents mentioned above, they usually insist on inspecting the tenant's financial statement. After all, the landlord and tenant are entering into a type of partnership. The landlord must feel confident that the tenant will stay and pay rent for the duration of the lease, especially if the landlord will provide the tenant with build-out for tenant improvements and other rental concessions.

A typical financial statement should contain a breakdown of assets, liabilities and net worth. Forms can be obtained from most lending institutions and office supply stores. If the tenant is just starting out in business, the landlord may require a personal financial statement as well.

Most landlords will want a personal and corporate credit check completed. This along with the financial statement will be studied before the landlord agrees to any lease terms or rental concessions.

IF YOU USE A REAL ESTATE BROKER

Whether a tenant should employ the services of a "buyer's broker" or "tenant representative" depends on the answers to the following questions:

- **TIME** - Can the business owner spare the time to search for all the possible locations?

- **EXPERIENCE** - Does the tenant have the experience to negotiate the best lease terms and concession package in the marketplace?

- **KNOWLEDGE** - Does the tenant understand all the financial implications of all the various lease clauses?

- **TEMPERAMENT** - Is the business owner skillful at negotiating for himself? Many people are skilled at negotiating for others, but find it difficult when it comes to negotiating for themselves.

Some real estate companies specialize in "tenant or buyer representation", and many of the nation's largest retailers hire these companies to represent them rather than use in-house personnel, or to work as a team with their in-house real estate department.

THREE WAYS TO WORK WITH
A REAL ESTATE BROKER

NOTE. In all of the following examples, it is the broker's duty and obligation to disclose to the parties involved who the broker is representing and how the broker is being paid. This should be in writing for the broker's protection, and to fulfill certain disclosure obligations required by the Real Estate Commission in various states. This should not cause a problem for tenant or landlord.

#1 LANDLORD'S BROKER, PAID BY LANDLORD

This is common, as when a tenant calls on a "For Lease" sign. In this case the broker obviously works for the landlord and is obligated to get the landlord the highest price possible for the space. Yes, tenant is "working with" a broker, they they are NOT being represented by one!

#2 TENANT'S BROKER, PAID BY LANDLORD

In this instance the tenant retains a real estate broker (on an exclusive or nonexclusive basis) for their site selection and/or lease negotiation process. The landlord in this case pays the broker's fee even though the broker is representing the tenant.

This legal and ethical way of doing business is a reflection of the realities of the marketplace.

Most landlords hire a leasing broker working on their behalf and who will receive a fee whether the tenant hires his own broker or not. USU-ALLY, the tenant's broker will share the leasing broker's fee, and there will be no increased cost to the transaction. When the tenant's broker is the first person to contact the landlord's broker, things go very smoothly. If the tenant has already started discussions with the landlord's broker and THEN brings the tenant's broker into the transaction, some friction can develop, at least temporarily.

#3 TENANT'S BROKER, PAID BY TENANT

There are several instances where tenants might directly pay a real estate broker:

A. If the client's volume of work encompasses most of the broker's time and attention. Many times the client will require the broker to complete various market studies, demographic studies, traffic studies, etc., in addition to the normal functions of locating sites and negotiating leases.

B. Tenant may have already found the location and may want the broker to negotiate a deal in his behalf.

In either of these situations the broker may still request payment from the landlord, but will be guaranteed a certain minimum amount per transaction by the tenant.

In other cases the broker is paid an hourly fee plus commissions or will require a retainer fee to start the site selection process. Following is a sample "tenant rep" agreement for study purposes.

AUTHORIZATION FOR BROKER REPRESENTATION
FACILITY ACQUISITIONS, DISPOSITIONS & LEASE RENEWALS
Sample for Study Purposes

This Agreement is by and between ___Business Owner_____ hereinafter referred to as "Client", and ___ABC Commercial Real Estate Company,___ hereinafter referred to as "Broker".

Client hereby requests Broker to use its experience and resources to: (a) Locate facilities appropriate for Client's use, (b) Dispose of any excess Client facilities, and (c) Negotiate the renewal of existing leases.

In consideration of the time, effort and expense spent by Broker, and other good and valuable consideration, the receipt and sufficiency of which is hereby acknowledged, Client hereby grants to Broker an exclusive right to represent Client as a Tenant/Buyer Representative in the purchase, sale or lease of real property, as described below.

1. BROKER'S DUTIES. Client hereby appoints Broker as its EXCLUSIVE BROKER to assist Client with its facilities needs throughout (County), (State) . Broker shall always act in Client's best interest in all relevant transactions, subject to Broker's legal duty, and shall not accept a "dual agency" role. Broker's duties include:

- Assist client with analyzing their specific space requirements, including future growth projections
- Performing Market Research to determine current prices, rates and terms for applicable properties
- Locating and reviewing all potential sites, facilities and/or acquisition possibilities, and analyzing same on client's behalf
- Submitting and negotiating Letters of Intent, Purchase Offers or Request for Proposals
- Reviewing and negotiating final lease or purchase documents (no legal advice)
- As applicable, obtain demographic studies, traffic studies, zoning and property information, and governmental incentive information

2. CLIENT'S DUTIES. Client will conduct all real estate negotiations and transactions specified in this contract exclusively with Broker during the term of this agreement, and any renewal period.

3. TERM. Broker's authority as Client's exclusive Broker shall commence immediately upon execution of this Agreement and shall terminate_____ months from said date, or 30 days after receipt by Broker of Client's written notice of termination. Notwithstanding the termination of this Agreement, the Broker's authority shall continue as to negotiations under way at time of such termination. During the term or after expiration, the term shall be considered to be automatically renewed for six months upon Client's notifying Broker of a new space requirement.

Either party may cancel this Agreement with 15 days written notice. Such termination shall not limit the Broker's right to commissions resulting from pending leases, sales or binding letters of intent which are not yet closed at time of termination.

If within 180 days after the termination of this contract, Client leases or acquires real property which had been submitted to Client by Broker or any other Third Party during the term of this contract, Client will be obligated to pay Broker's Fee.

4. BROKER'S COMPENSATION. (strike out any that do not apply**)**

LEASE or PURCHASE of new land or facility: Broker's compensation shall be a Brokerage Fee paid by the Listing Broker, Seller or Landlord. If the Seller or Landlord will not pay a fee, then Client may either pay fee to Broker or decline to purchase or lease the property. Said fee is a minimum of ____ Percent (__%) of the gross sales price for Sales Transactions, or ___% of the aggregate Gross Lease amount (yearly Base Rent and Pass-Thru Expenses times number of years of lease) for Lease transactions. This fee is earned and payable when client enters into a written binding lease or purchase contract.

LEASE RENEWALS OR RENEGOTIATIONS: Broker shall attempt to obtain payment for services from the Landlord. If the Landlord will not compensate Broker, then Client agrees to pay Broker an amount equal to ___% of the total amount saved from the existing lease or renewal option, or benefits received. Savings and benefits to the Tenant shall be determined and defined as: (a) The difference between the proposed/existing option renewal rate and the rate re-negotiated by the Broker, or the difference between the existing rental rate and the rate negotiated by Broker. (Existing rental rates shall include base rental and all other building and operating expenses.), and (b) Tenant finish dollars, rental abatement or other inducements that equate to dollars saved or earned and provided by Landlord. These benefits and savings shall be the aggregate received over the lease term.

<u>DISPOSITIONS (SALE or LEASE OF PROPERTY)</u>: If and when satisfactory Lease and Purchase Agreements are entered into between Client and Purchaser/Lessee, Client shall pay to Broker a commission equal to the following:

Leases - A Leasing Commission of ____ Percent (__%) of the Initial Lease Term and __% of any extensions or renewals. ("Initial Lease Term" = yearly base rent times number of years). Fees shall be due Fifty Percent (50%) upon Lease Execution and Fifty Percent (50%) upon Lease Commencement. (These fees shall be shared with cooperating brokers.)

Sales - A Sales Commission of ____ Percent (__%) of the total purchase price. Fees shall be considered earned upon final execution of Purchase Agreement and shall be paid at closing. If after the negotiations have been completed and agreed to bi-laterally by Client and Purchaser, the sale fails to close as a result of Client's actions or failure to act, then any Broker's Fee that would have been paid will be immediately due and payable by Client. (These fees shall be shared with cooperating brokers.)

Upon execution of this Agreement, Client does hereby submit a retainer in the amount of $_____, which shall be non-refundable and applied towards the first Fees due to Broker by Client, or reimbursed to Client at the closing of a successful transaction.

Other than the compensation stated above, Broker shall accept no other compensation, incentive, bonus, rebate or other consideration without the client's express knowledge and acceptance.

5. MISCELLANEOUS.
(a) Client acknowledges Broker does not offer legal advice, and agrees to seek outside legal counsel as necessary.
(b) This contract shall inure to the benefit of and be binding upon the parties hereto and their respective personal representatives, guardians, assignees, purchasers, subsidiaries, affiliates and successors. No assignment of Client's rights under this contract and no assignment of rights in this property obtained for Client under this contract shall operate to defeat any of Broker's rights.
(c) Broker shall attempt to insure all information and documents relative to the Project are accurate and complete to the best of Broker's knowledge, however Client agrees to indemnify and hold Broker harmless from damages resulting from omissions or inaccuracy of said information.
(d) All notices to each party shall be forwarded using a return receipt, or acknowledgement of receipt, by any commonly accepted method.

6. LITIGATION. Parties agree that with regard to any litigation, including appellate proceedings arising out of this agreement, the prevailing party shall be entitled to recover reasonable attorney's fees and costs. This Agreement shall be governed by the laws of the State of _____ as to interpretation, construction, and performance. Venue shall be in _____ County, (state).

Broker shall conduct all Brokerage activities without respect to the race, color, religion, sex, national origin, handicap or familial status of any party or prospective party to the agreement.

The parties below warrant they have the legal capacity, right and authority to bind their respective companies to this Agreement.

Agreed and Accepted:
CLIENT:

X_____   Date _____

BROKER:

X_____   Date _____

FIGURING THE FEES

Most tenants do not know or care how much commission their broker is being paid, but for those curious few, leasing fees are generally figured in one of two ways:

1. **PERCENTAGE OF LEASE TERM.** This is a fee that is calculated as a percentage of the total income that the landlord will receive from the tenant during the term of the lease. Option periods are sometimes calculated in, although oftentimes at a reduced percentage.

2. **RATE PER SQUARE FOOT LEASED.** This is simply an agreed upon rate that the landlord will pay to broker based on the SIZE of the space leased.

The time of payment of the fee is also negotiable. While some brokers may demand the full fee to be paid at final lease execution, others will wait until occupancy or split the fee, some due at signing and some due at occupancy. Other times the landlord may insist that the final portion of the lease payment not be made until the tenant has "seasoned", or has been in the property a portion of time to make sure he is going to "make it". Still others, especially when the fee is large, will pay it monthly, quarterly or yearly over the life of the lease.

FINAL SUMMARY–*NO MORE MYSTERY!*

Done carefully and with the proper research and knowledge, selecting the best site and negotiating the best lease terms are simple and attainable goals. The most astute business owners will not trust to luck in their selection of locations any more than they would trust to luck in the ingredients they put into their products or the pricing they place on those products.

Proper Site Selection is a key ingredient of success, and even a cursory analysis of successful businesses will prove this point.

Whether business owners do the site analysis research and sales/lease negotiation themselves or whether they hire professionals, they will find that the right facility, in the right location, at the right price will multiply the effectiveness of their other efforts.

For more information contact:

www.LeaseSmart.com

Craig A. Melby, CCIM

(828) 884-4454

TOP 10
Lease Negotiation & Site Selection
MISTAKES

Craig Melby, CCIM

Following are the Top 10 mistakes companies make when searching for new space. The content and rankings are the result of a survey taken among experienced practitioners in the Lease Negotiation field. Each participant in the survey was a senior principal in their company, and averaged over 20 years of experience in the Site Selection, Lease Negotiation and Facility Acquisition field.

 # NOT ALLOWING ENOUGH TIME

This was far and away the top mistake companies make: *Starting Too Late!* It takes TIME to research the market and qualify all the possible sites or facility choices, then tour the properties which seem most interesting, and then compare them carefully. While this CAN be completed in as little as a week or so by motivated companies already familiar with the local market, the normal time to do this would be more like a month, especially if you intend to allow time to hear back from Brokers and Owners on "unlisted" properties: those properties where a Tenant is in place, but could move out (or be moved out) if a replacement occupant is found. Even then, these tasks are only the *tip* of the "time drain" iceberg. Other tasks that need to be factored into the relocation time-line include:

- **Negotiations.** Typically done with Letters Of Intent (LOIs) or Requests For Proposal (RFPs), negotiations with the Landlord can span weeks or even months if the landlord is a big company with a real estate committee that meets once a week. Terms are battered back and forth like a tennis ball. Perhaps bids need to be obtained for various items before either Landlord or Tenant will agree to certain work. It is not unusual for things to seem to drag on forever.

- **Preparation of the lease.** Once the financial terms are agreed upon, a new round of negotiations commences: the principals, brokers and attorneys need to battle back and forth over the wording of the lease, and the "devilish-details" can easily bring up new issues of disagreement that need resolution. This can easily take weeks.

- **Renovations.** Once the lease is signed the premises often needs finishing or renovating, which can add additional months. Rooms are never the right size, and even when they are, you may want a different style of floor plan. If it's an open floor plan, YOU want private offices, or vice versa. Happens all the time! I have seen offices installed exactly the way they used to be - before the most recent tenant ripped everything out to make an open floor plan.

- **Permits.** Before renovations can begin, building permits must be obtained. This will take additional weeks – perhaps much longer if the municipality is "backed up", and don't forget it is common for plans to be rejected for one reason or another and require revisions, and then resubmission.

- **Architectural plans**. Need building permits? Then you need architectural plans! How busy is the architect and how detailed are the drawings? This can easily take one to two months. If the architect is busy it may be a month before he/she can START the work.

Bottom line: Unless existing facilities can be found with the right floor plan and features, the process with renovations can easily take 9 months to a year - horror stories abound in the industry of it taking even longer. Depending on the size and complexity of the transaction, six months to a year is a reasonable time frame to use when looking for new facilities – and longer is necessary if you think you may have to build from ground up. Expect the process to take even longer if experienced planners are not retained to guide the process, since it is likely you will commence the process with an incomplete amount of governmental issues and forms addressed.

NEGLECTING LONG-TERM PRIORITIES

Business owners who think only about solving immediate needs may face expansion or relocation problems again very soon. In addition to evaluating short term needs like size requirements, type of floor plan (open, private, or a mixture), communications needs, parking needs, access, amenities, and security needs, etc., be sure to factor in long term and "what if" needs. What happens if you decide to acquire another company, or get an offer to BE acquired? Will your long-term lease obligation stand in the way? Smart companies will obtain *facilities* and *lease terms* which will allow the company to expand, downsize or relocate as circumstances dictate. Experienced business owners do their best to avoid unnecessary headaches, loss of business and costs associated with relocating.

Examples of important lease clauses include:

- **Expansion right**. The Landlord is obligated to provide the tenant with more space should it become necessary. If Landlord can't provide the space, tenant may give notice and cancel the lease.

- **Cancellation right.** Commonly referred to as a "kick-out" clause, this language allows the tenant to break the lease under certain conditions such as when the tenant suffers a certain level of loss in sales or business, or sales and growth don't meet expectations.

- **Renewal Option.** The more the better as you don't HAVE to exercise them unless they are to your advantage.

- **Extension right**. Similar to a renewal option and allows the tenant to remain in the premises (a right of first refusal is a type of extension right).

- Sublet right gives the Tenant flexibility in that if it must relocate, it may sublease the space and mitigate the economic pressure of the ongoing lease payments.

Suggestion: After discussing the company's immediate needs and long terms goals with senior management in all departments, meet with leasing experts and space planners/architects to determine:

- *The most productive combination of office size and layouts (modular furniture, hoteling, size, amenity requirements, etc.)*
- *Buildings which are big and flexible enough to service future needs*
- *Certain lease clauses which will be negotiated into the lease document*

INADEQUATE REPRESENTATION

Sorry this sounds a bit self-serving coming from a Tenant Representative, but hey – it really *was* the third most common mistake and we're committed to printing the absolute truth whether or not it happens to be to our advantage or disadvantage! I am not surprised this came I so high as I personally hear horror stories about this all the time. Unless someone in the company is already an expert in commercial real estate, business owners cannot afford the time necessary to learn this complicated industry to a high enough level, and they almost always leave money on the table, and"land-mines" in the lease. Real quick: Do you know the difference between a Gross Lease, Net Lease and Full Service Lease? How about "T.I." and Incentives? Lack of knowledge combined with time pressures can cause unrepresented owners to make location decisions without being

Business owners who do not use a Broker will not be aware of ALL the possible facility choices since many properties are not on the "open" market. Perhaps the best space isn't vacant yet, but will be coming available soon. Great spaces may have Tenants in them who would like to vacate if a replacement Tenant could be found.

Who is going to counterbalance the Landlord's professionals, and insure the Business Owner finds the best space and receives the best possible rates, terms, incentives and lease clause protections. Most Landlord representatives are wonderful, nice people. But their JOB is to get the best possible deal for the Landlord. Incredibly, this valuable service usually costs the business owner nothing, since Tenant Reps usually share in the Leasing fees paid by the Landlord.

Got a friend in the business? Using the *wrong* broker may still lead to inexperience induced errors, incomplete information or even conflicting loyalties because of hidden agendas or Landlord relationships.

Suggestion: *Business owners should also keep their Broker involved in the expansions, contractions, renewals and extensions that occur during the lease to prevent uninformed decisions that lead to lost opportunities. Renewals are a negotiable event! Don't just sign the extension blindly.*

LEASE COMMENCEMENT DATE NOT TIED TO PREMISES COMPLETION

This is a disaster when inexperienced Business Owners find that unexpected delays in the planning, permitting or construction stages have eaten into their rent-free build-out period and caused budget nightmares. In fact, I know of a business which went out-of-business before they even opened! It simply took too long and cost too much to get the space ready, and they ran out of money.

Suggestion: Business owners should always propose a clause to the lease which provides for an extension of the lease commencement date if pre-opening delays are encountered which are beyond the business owner's control. Or my favorite choice, depending on circumstances: Make it the Landlord's responsibility to bring the space to a certain level of readiness. Cost or time overruns? That's the Landlord's problem!

 ## UNDERESTIMATING THE CONDITION OF THE PREMISES

Tenants who take a property "as is" put themselves at great risk. Even when the space looks fine and has been previously occupied, building codes may have changed or the unit's infrastructure could be broken or inadequate. Watch for latent defects and hidden problems. These issues may be unknown even to the Landlord so it is not an honesty issue. The issue is WHO is responsible to fix them when they are discovered.

Suggestion: It is best to have the Landlord guarantee that the space is up to current building, fire, safety, zoning and Americans with Disability Act (ADA) codes. The Landlord should also guarantee the condition of the electrical, plumbing, heating and air-conditioning systems for the first 60 to 90 days (if not the entire term of the lease.)

 ## USING THE LANDLORD'S PROFESSIONALS

Tenants should be very careful about using the Landlord's professionals, whose loyalty is to the Landlord. Business owners may find it money well spent to hire space planners, architects, general contractors and legal counsel under their control to create and review the various space plans, specifications, costs, and documents. Otherwise, the tenant may receive inferior and/or bloated designs and/or fixtures that are less efficient and could dramatically increase yearly operating costs.

Remember: excess rent comes right off the bottom line, and renting even 15% more space than you really need can offset a lot of hard-earned sales.

⑦ MISUNDERSTANDING THE TRUE SPACE COSTS

Business owners who are inexperienced with commercial real estate are often unable to perform true "apples to apples" analysis when comparing different facility choices. It can be complicated, even for the professional, to compare the different lease types in different buildings (i.e. Full Service, Gross, Semi-Gross, Net, Triple Net, etc.) Additionally, the following factors should be part of the comparison equation: the Landlord's interior finish levels, Tenant Improvement (TI) contributions, and lease incentives. The confusion and myriad of things to consider leads many owners to make less than optimum decisions. (To further complicate matters, in MY opinion the final dollar in rent shouldn't be the deciding factor anyway. I believe the costs of hiring, training and retaining good employees far outweighs many differences in rental cost between a facility that makes your employees happy and productive, and one which causes more turnover. Not to mention the importance of attracting more customers!)

⑧ PAYING TOO MUCH RENT/ NOT ENOUGH LANDLORD INCENTIVES

I once obtained $17,000 in build-out costs for a client, which was a complete surprise to him! When he was reading the final lease prior to execution he called me to ask, "What's this $17,000 for?" I said, "Its money the Landlord is reimbursing you towards your new paint and carpet expense". He says, "Why would the landlord DO that?", and I replied, "Because I asked him to!"

Business Owners that do not obtain accurate, current, market research may pay too high a rental rate or receive too few incentives, including benefits like free rent before and after lease commencement, discounted rent for various time periods, Landlord contributions to tenant's build-out costs, landlord improvements to the space, limits on future rent increases, etc.

102

Date:_____

_____ **$ Too Much**

_____Dollars

A Landlord's "flexibility" changes constantly depending upon many factors including current occupancy rates in both their building and the competition, lease length, tenant's use, parking requirements, financial strength of tenant, etc. Negotiations are also important with lease renewals, since Landlords are most competitive when the space is vacant, or may become vacant, if they don't deal with you based on market conditions.

NO DISASTER PLANNING

Think of the havoc wreaked if a hurricane or fire destroys all or part of your premises. Most Business Owners do not realize many leases allow Landlords unlimited time to rebuild the premises, and the Tenant must return once the space is ready. Although rent may be abated during this period, the Tenant is NOT free to lease other space and get on with business. This "out-of-order" period would be a fatal blow to many businesses.

NO OUTSIDE INCENTIVES

How about 30 MILLION Dollars? That's how much EXTRA one Tenant Representative brought to a client. Nice surprise, huh?

When a company expands or relocates to a new region, it may be possible to obtain substantial economic incentives from local and state government. Incentives can be tax rebates, relocation assistance, payroll subsidies during employee training, infrastructure improvements and others. Many times the statutory incentives can be negotiated up very substantially and an inexperienced company will almost always leave money on the table – sometimes in the millions of dollars! It's all about jobs. The number of jobs, type of jobs and pay scale of the jobs, and the prestige of the company moving to the area – and getting the local or state government to negotiate with you for your business.

Suggestion: *Use an experienced "location analyst and incentive negotiator" to make sure you obtain the best incentives possible.*

We hope you have found this material useful. There are plenty more common mistakes companies make but it would take volumes to discuss. More free information and videos on Lease Negotiation and Site Selection can be found on our website: www.LeaseSmart.com

If you'd like personal help, and want to put our 30+ years of experience to work for you and make the facility acquisition process painless, give us a call.

Craig Melby, CCIM • (800) 962-2419 • cmelby@ccim.net
www.TheMelbyGroup.com
www.LeaseSmart.com

Made in the USA
San Bernardino, CA
31 March 2019